RAPD
TEAMWORK

5 Steps to
Transform Groups
into Great Teams

Sean Glaze

TABLE OF CONTENTS

PREFACE
WHY READ THIS BOOK?

◆

ACCORDING TO MOST EDUCATED ESTIMATES, it took around 30 years to build the Great Pyramid at Giza. Great things, we have been told, always take time.

Rome was not built in a day . . .

You can likely think of countless other examples that warn not to expect overnight success.

And Eddie Cantor would agree.

He was a celebrated comedian, dancer, singer, actor and songwriter who performed on Broadway and in the early years of Hollywood. Cantor is credited with saying, "It takes 20 years to make an overnight success."

Just like building the great pyramid, most people believe that building great teams take lots and lots of time. But we are living in a microwave society now.

You are impatient.

You want to get things built faster than they built the Great Pyramid.

Success in business or athletics or academics isn't measured over decades . . .

Today, you will likely be judged by the way your teams perform over only a period few months.

And to have that rapid success and meet those increasingly time-sensitive expectations, you need to be able to build teams *more quickly and more effectively*.

That's why you want to **read this book**!

This book is valuable, because it shrinks your learning curve.

Instead of requiring the 15 years of tough lessons that I endured while learning the recipe that allowed talented teams to thrive together, you can steal my recipe and implement the ideas within these pages and enjoy the benefits of Rapid Teamwork without having to pay the price of wrong decisions, frustrations, and wasted time that accompanied my learning process.

I have found that speed is just as important as skill. Knowing HOW to do something is only useful if you can learn it on time to take advantage of and benefit from that information.

The wisest leaders in any industry are able to learn from the mistakes of others and emulate the processes and philosophies that led to other's achievements.

The story in the pages that follow shares a recipe of five commitments that you can begin to apply immediately to build a higher performing team – faster than most would assume possible.

You really can have **Rapid Teamwork**!

Careers used to be 30 years, now projects last less than 30 months. In modern corporate and medical fields, there is a revolving door of employees and teammates…

Leaders must be able to build teams that function well together and create a sense of unity and rapport and supportive collaboration. Thankfully, GREAT teams aren't pyramids – they can be built quickly and effectively.

Great teams are the result of learning and then focusing on following a proven recipe for success.

Your organization's productivity can change just as dramatically, if you choose to implement the powerful set of five commitments that are described within these pages. Rapid Teamwork – in athletics, in business, in education, in healthcare, in sales, and in virtually any other industry – is achievable by following the formula laid out in the parable that follows.

I hope you will enjoy the story –

More importantly, I hope you will apply its lessons to your organization – and enjoy the GREAT results that this proven recipe will produce...

CHAPTER 1

ANOTHER MORNING

"GREAT."

He shrugged his shoulders and let out a sigh.

"That's just great."

Greg Sharpe fell back into his seat and slapped the side of his truck's steering wheel with his thick left hand.

He pushed the gas pedal and then hunched forward one last time to turn the key again . . . but there was absolutely no response at all from the engine.

"You gotta be kidding me," he complained.

He yanked his keys from the ignition and exploded out of the driver's seat. His shoes had not even hit the driveway before he began yelling for his wife.

"Honey!" He took another deep breath and moved in long determined strides back toward their front door, glancing down at his watch as the digital numbers continued to turn more quickly than he would like toward 8:00 am.

"Honey – The truck…" But instead of grabbing the door handle and turning it, he stopped himself.

Lisa was still asleep after being up to comfort their 10-year-old daughter, who was having nightmares about a scary movie trailer she had seen a few nights ago on the television.

He needed to figure this out himself.

Moving quickly back to the 2010 Dodge Ram pickup, he reached inside and pulled the hood latch, then walked to the front of the truck to see if there was anything his untrained eye could identify as the issue.

After propping up the hood, his eyes focused on the battery terminals.

They were corroded and caked over with white stuff. He went inside, filled a 32 ounce plastic cup with warm water and grabbed the baking soda, and returned in a half sprint to pour them over the top of the neglected battery.

When it finished fizzing, he could feel that the end of the positive cable was loose, so he attacked it furiously with a wrench, and after a few rushed twists to tighten it up he pulled his keys from the front pocket of his shorts and inserted one of them back into the ignition.

He paused a moment to pray an urgent selfish prayer, and turned the key.

The engine roared to life.

He smiled weakly, still frustrated with the inconvenience of his Saturday morning surprise, but proud to have found the solution.

He glanced back at his watch again as he put the vehicle in reverse to back out of the driveway, and saw that it was already 7:52 am.

He wouldn't be early, but he would at least make it there, nearly on time.

When he pulled into the parking lot in front of the warehouse, Keith Johnson was waiting outside the door.

Greg did not make it a habit of showing up anywhere late – it drove him nuts – but this morning his being a minute or two late was the least of his worries.

Following the location's last financial report, he was not going to get upset about being a minute or two late to meet his inventory guy. If he was going to get upset, it would be because he didn't feel like the last six weeks of meetings had created the focus or positive energy he had hoped to inspire.

Heck . . . this morning was just one big metaphor for the company he was supposed to be leading.

Loose connections.

No energy.

The people at CDI were just not a close team.

And like his truck, the pieces were all in good shape, but they still didn't seem to click.

Just yesterday, he had gotten word that one of his sales team planned to transfer to work for a competitor. Maybe the office needed a jolt of something different. He just didn't know what.

"Morning, Mister Sharpe!"

"Morning, Keith. You been waiting long?"

"No, sir. Just a minute or two."

That was probably a white lie. More than any of his employees, Keith was always early to appointments.

"Thought I had a dead truck, but it was just something with the battery."

Greg Sharpe unlocked the door and motioned for his inventory manager to go in first.

Keith walked inside first, turning on lights and then peeking into an office to grab a clipboard off the crowd of papers and folders on the desk.

"You do anything last night with the group?"

Keith was occasionally a good source of information about what many other employees were feeling or thinking.

"Not really. I hung out for a while watching the game with Patrick at J.D.'s. There were a couple of others there, but that was it. We split before halftime, though. I was tired."

Tired didn't usually keep younger guys from having a good time on a Friday night, Greg thought. Certainly not, after annual reviews had just ended.

If they weren't blowing off steam together last night, then really there were problems between some of the employees. And it certainly didn't make Greg happy to hear that many of them had begun to congregate at J.D.'s.

Greg knew that J.D. Cornett was one of the more charismatic sales people on staff, and he was certainly talented. But being a charismatic leader didn't mean that someone would always lead people in the best direction.

Sharpe had hoped that Patrick Perkins, a designer he had hired about the same time Cornett was, and Keith Johnson, the dependable and ambitious warehouse worker who had joined him for inventory review this morning, would help with improving the culture – but his idealistic hopes weren't always reflected in reality.

Positions can be assigned – but leadership is always earned.

J.D. was apparently one of the more influential voices in the company, and that could be a challenging situation.

"Good," Greg replied, "Nice to have you guys spending time together and staying out of trouble!"

Sharpe's voice did not sound as enthusiastic as he had intended.

"Thanks again for giving up your Saturday morning to come in and help with inventory. I'm glad you're here."

Keith nodded, and pointed at the clipboard he was holding that listed all of the furniture and other items that should be there on site.

Annual reviews had mostly focused on two things – processes and performance.

It was a chance for the director of each division to teach more about the changes and tools they had implemented to make things better, and it allowed each employee to hear how they had done according to the new metrics that had been put into place to boost the productivity.

Sharpe had done his first inventory alone over a year ago. He had enjoyed the peace and quiet and the opportunity to process his thoughts about taking over as general manager.

But when Keith offered to join him and help with the paperwork part of things, Sharpe felt it might be a nice change – not to mention that Keith was very organized and would likely make it go smoothly and take much less time.

The two worked well together, talking about some of the recent changes at CDI, some of the challenges and opportunities that next year would bring, and about Keith's plans for the future.

After nearly two hours had passed, with almost everything having been accounted for, Greg returned to the topic of his employees and their feelings about the company...

Keith's words became a bit more careful.

"I know what you're wondering, Mister Sharpe. I do. And I think it'll be okay."

Keith looked down at the clipboard and paused, then continued to talk. Sharpe kept looking at the shelves full of large boxes, but was listening intently.

"It's only a couple of people that are complaining. And the stuff a couple of days ago with J.D. was kinda weird, but next month it won't mean nothin."

The "stuff" that Keith referred to was a verbal confrontation in the middle of their offices last Wednesday. It was a rough afternoon and people had been working to find out what had happened to a few items that one of their recent clients called about.

According to the client, the items had not been installed and there was nobody from CDI there on site. Greg had let his frustration get the best of him, but there was never an excuse for employee insubordination.

It had been a three-hour ordeal of tracking down the installers and ensuring the client was taken care of. What Sharpe had done in barking at J.D. was not just an emotional reaction to the stress of dealing with an unhappy client, or the added aggravation of employees who had been slow to adapt to his leadership – it was, to him, a necessary consequence.

He assured himself that his outburst at J.D. was a defining moment of discipline.

Greg Sharpe wholeheartedly believed in the mantra he had learned from one of his high school coaches: discipline determines victory – and the greater the discipline, the greater the eventual victory. Changing times were an illusion . . . people, whether athletes or employees, would always benefit from firm guardrails.

Yes, there was frustration in all of them from the last quarter's underwhelming financial report.

But, spring was supposed to be a time of rebirth and renewed hope . . .

That was part of what the annual reviews were about – looking back in order to look ahead in anticipation of what might be accomplished and enjoyed and accomplished in the future.

But part of what had led to his outburst with J.D. was the frustration that most of the employees seemed less than enthusiastic during their individual meetings.

And Greg didn't know what to do.

So in the midst of that unexpected client issue, he stood in the middle of the office, wondering how the installers and inventory guys and designers could have allowed this to happen, and said in a more booming tone than he meant to use that "people here need to do a better job of talking to each other and sharing information!"

After he said it, his collar felt tight.

He was angry with concern . . . and now was upset with himself.

And at that very moment he noticed J.D. exaggerate an eye-roll and a scowl.

Sharpe let the last eighteen months of frustration trying to improve processes and increase profits at this new location, exacerbated by the employee conflicts and communication issues, get the best of him.

He didn't raise his voice very often, but at that moment he turned J.D.'s disrespectful reaction into a referendum on his leadership.

He stared at J.D., one of the company's most veteran salespeople, then barked, "And if anybody has a problem with the changes we're making, we can definitely change more than metrics and processes!"

Afterwards, Greg withdrew into his office for the afternoon. It had not been one of his better moments.

He looked up from his thoughts and motioned for Keith to let him hold the clipboard.

"Hey, Keith – you've been a big help, but I can finish this up myself. Go enjoy the rest of your weekend."

Keith looked at him with a bit of concern. "You sure, Mister Sharpe?

"Yeah . . . I need to make sure that the..."

In the middle of his sentence, "Rocky Top" startled him, blaring from inside the front pocket of his shorts. It was the ringtone from his phone.

Greg grabbed for his phone to take the call and just waved and nodded goodbye to Keith, who understood and left the warehouse as he answered it.

"Hello...?"

"Hi there, handsome."

"Hey, honey. Kids okay?"

"Yes . . . just missing you. How much longer before you're done?"

"Not too long. I almost woke you up this morning."

"Oh?"

"Yeah – Truck wouldn't start. Turned out the battery connections were bad. I took care of it. Did you get to sleep in some?"

"A little. See you for a late lunch, maybe?"

"Sure. I'll call you on my way."

"Okay. Love you!"

"You too."

Just as he flipped the phone closed to hang up and slid it back into his pocket, "Rocky Top" rang out again.

He was sure he knew exactly why she was calling back.

"Hey baby – what is it you need me to pick up?"

"Mister Sharpe?"

It was not his wife's voice.

"Uh . . . yes . . . sorry . . . Who is this?"

"This is Anne Cassidy. Mr. Patterson's secretary...?"

"Oh. Good morning, Ms. Cassidy."

Matthew Patterson was the president of CDI National.

Patterson had been in that position for less than six months, but Ms. Cassidy had been at the company for years, and had actually welcomed Greg to the president's office three years ago when he had interviewed for the general manager position at their Nashville location.

Sharpe had said hello to the new president on a couple of occasions, but they had never shared much more than brief conversations and professional handshakes.

"I understand it is a Saturday, but Mr. Patterson is there in town and would like to meet with you this afternoon, at your offices, if you are available."

"Oh . . . Okay." Greg's thoughts were all over the place, then he collected himself. "Yes, I can meet with him later today. What time did he have in mind?"

"He has a two-o'clock opening if you can make it, or he could see you after five."

"Let's make it at two."

"Terrific. I'll pencil you in . . . He'll see you after lunch, Mr. Sharpe."

"Yes, ma'am."

Greg had no idea what the meeting was going to focus on.

Maybe it was just a chance to get to know each other better. Having been hired by the previous president of the company, he knew that this call would come eventually, and hoped it was just an attempt by the new guy to learn more about the people who worked for him.

But as a relatively new location general manager, he didn't yet feel completely secure in his job.

You never knew what the next guy in charge would think was important, or how interested he was in doing things HIS way with HIS people.

So going to meet the new president with his location's numbers still hovering somewhere near the middle of the pack for each of the last five quarters made Sharpe a bit uneasy.

On his way back home, he made two calls.

First, he called to ask his wife if she could have a sandwich waiting for him, and told her about the appointment he had just accepted.

After that, at a red light he scrolled down his list of contacts to find his brother in law's name, and called him. A little advice from Ben wouldn't hurt.

But there was no answer.

Greg left a voice mail that said simply, "hey . . . gimme a call back."

He allowed his mind to explore a few upsetting possibilities about what the meeting's purpose might be.

He pulled into his driveway muttering the same word to himself that he had hours ago that morning. He was more and more worried about this meeting, and bothered by the feeling he had about his location's performance.

Sharpe was upset, and had a habit when he was upset of biting his lower lip, letting out heavy sighs through his nose, and shaking his head . . .

This was all followed by a one-word attempt to express his exasperation.

"Great!"

CHAPTER 2

AN UNCOMFORTABLE CONVERSATION

THERE WAS A HAM and Swiss sandwich on the kitchen counter for him when he walked inside, and his wife was standing by the sink, smiling.

"You worry too much."

"Think you know me pretty well, do you?" he replied.

"After 14 years . . . I think so. Did you call Ben?"

Maybe Lisa did know him better than he thought. He didn't answer her.

He waved and flashed a smile at his daughter in the living room, who waved back and quickly returned her attention to the television where she was watching something on the Disney Channel.

"Well, I love you. And I'm sure he's going to like you just fine. Go in, expecting it to be a good meeting, okay? Don't spend the next half hour being anxious."

"Thanks baby."

"So . . . what did Ben say?"

"Ha... I haven't talked with Ben, miss know-it-all."

He smiled at her and took another bite of the sandwich.

Then the sound of "Rocky Top" filled the kitchen.

Lisa chuckled and pointed at her husband's pocket. "Tell Ben his little sister said hi…"

Greg walked out of the kitchen and into their living room to get away from the sound of the television. "Hello?"

"Hey buddy. What's up?"

It was Ben.

"Well, it's probably nothing. But, I wanted to know what you thought."

"Okay…"

"I've been invited to a two o'clock meeting with the new president. His secretary didn't say what it was about. It's probably just to get to know each other better. But I wondered if you thought I…"

"Well, Greg, my situation is a little different," Ben interrupted.

There was a part of Greg that wished he hadn't called.

Yes, Ben's situation was definitely different. Instead of having to struggle through the pressures and consequences of leading employees and running an actual business, Ben was used to giving advice with impunity.

Ben Cooper, Greg's brother in law, had left a telecom management position to become a strategic planning consultant fifteen years before, when his college buddy called and offered a position in his consulting firm.

And as much as Greg appreciated having the knowledge of someone who was familiar with CRM and SWOT and Benchmarking to talk about things like this, his pride often got in the way.

And while he had gotten close enough to Ben to know that he was genuinely glad to share any ideas or wisdom he could, there was a part of himself that bristled, when Ben spoke and perceived an arrogance in his voice.

"Right. Well, Patterson wants to see me at two. Anything I should go in prepared to say or talk about, you think?"

There was a short pause on the other end of the line.

"What do the comparable store sales figures look like?"

Greg thought a moment. "I don't know if it's about stuff like that. His secretary didn't ask me to put together any numbers. Of course, nobody likes plateaus, but we're doing okay."

"Well – if your location numbers aren't growing, I imagine the new guy is aware of that. But maybe it is just to say hello now he's gotten settled into the position."

"I guess so. Maybe."

"Have you talked with your directors? Maybe they've heard something. Gimme a call this evening to let me know how it went, okay?"

"You got it. And I want to ask you something else about the sales quota stuff we talked about, too. Still have a couple more things I want to understand better before we implement them. Make sure we set ourselves up for a strong summer."

"Alright Greg. Talk to you later."

"Bye."

Before he put the phone back into his pocket, he looked at the screen to check the time.

It was just past 1:00, and he needed to get back over to the sales office soon.

He jogged upstairs to brush his teeth. He tucked his red polo shirt with the CDI logo back neatly into his khakis, brushed through his thinning brown hair, and made his way back down the steps.

Greg smiled at his wife as he went back into the kitchen.

"Okay . . . so you know me pretty well."

She wrapped her arms around his neck. "And somehow I still love you!"

He kissed her and said he would be back as soon as the meeting was over, and she continued to watch him through the window as he pulled out of the driveway and drove off.

He reached the sales offices a few minutes later. One of the perks of living and working in Nashville was that everything was less than twenty minutes away.

The shiny steel door swung smoothly open as he pulled on the decorative brass handle, and Greg Sharpe made his way down the hall to wait for the president's visit.

It was a large two-story silver and glass building – and Greg had been responsible for the people and the profits of that location for almost two years now. This was the first time, though, that the new president of Commercial Design and Interiors had made the trip for a chat.

It was only a few minutes later that Matthew Patterson walked through the door. He strode in confidently while extending his hand to greet the Nashville CDI general manager.

Greg stood up and met him in the showroom area, offering a firm handshake and warm smile to his boss.

After a few short comments about the weather and other small talk, Matthew Patterson grabbed a legal pad from his desk and asked Greg if he would like to sit down – he pointed to one of the model tables that was surrounded by four modern but comfortable chairs.

Patterson was wearing a dark blue suit with a white dress shirt and no tie. Greg noticed a silver pin on his lapel that looked like a "U," but didn't ask about it.

"Greg, I really appreciate you coming in today . . . I've been trying to meet with most of the location managers and directors to get a feel from as many people as possible about where our company is and what I can do to keep us all moving in the right direction."

"I'm happy to be here, Mr. Patterson."

"Good! Let's have a seat."

They both sat down.

"Greg, I usually try to schedule these ahead of time, and I like to send ahead a list of three questions that ask people to answer before our meeting." Patterson paused, but only to catch his breath and adjust his suit jacket before continuing.

"The questions are simple. I ask them to tell me what they think their department needs to do less of, what they think they need to start doing more of, and what their department needs my help with in order to get better."

"Okay…"

Greg was unsure if he was supposed to think of an answer now or not.

"But with our similar backgrounds, I thought it might be better if I went about things a little differently with you."

Greg was glad to feel like he was off the hook for the moment, and waited politely for the president to continue.

"So, I'll start by asking you this. How do YOU think things are going with our Nashville location?"

Greg hesitated, unsure exactly what he should say.

That was such a broad question.

"Well, we're doing okay. Profits are still good… No arrests this week."

He hoped that might draw a smile from Mr. Patterson, but Patterson listened without much response or emotion.

"And we're looking forward to next quarter. Have a bunch of projects in the pipeline, and I think our people are getting used to some of the changes we made…"

His voice trailed off and he waited for a response.

Mr. Patterson nodded and leaned forward to put his legal pad and pen back on the table.

"Greg, how much do you know about me?"

Sharpe realized he really didn't know very much about the man at all.

He had read the newspaper story announcing his hiring after Daniels' retirement, and he had heard bits and pieces about his background as a coach and then moved into sales and climb to CEO at another company, but hadn't really done any extra digging beyond the press releases and company emails.

"Just what's on the 'about us' web page, I guess. And what I heard from you at the last annual meeting where you introduced yourself from the stage and shared your goals."

"Did you know that years ago I was a coach, too?"

Greg couldn't wait to hear where this was going.

"Basketball, right?"

"That's right. Played my way through college, then I got into coaching. Other than my father, the one man that had the greatest impact on my life was a coach I had while I was in high school. Athletics can be a tremendous classroom for teaching leadership."

"I think so, too," Greg said. "Hopefully our people here benefit from that. The one thing I shared with President Daniels when I first interviewed for the job was that I would always emphasize three C's – competence, character, and competition."

Patterson nodded and leaned back for a moment in his chair, leaning on the right arm rest.

"Greg, you don't want me wasting our time, do you?"

"No, I don't guess so."

"Good – because I think something needs to change."

Greg swallowed uncomfortably.

"What do you mean?" Certainly he wasn't being fired?

"By all accounts, Greg, you have a good heart and want to succeed and push your people to perform and meet expectations. In fact, every bit of the asking around I've done has confirmed that you are a man of character who works very hard. I want you to know that I appreciate that very much."

Greg was a bit confused now.

"So what do you think that needs to change?"

"Well, that's why I called you in today. I'm hoping you can figure that out for us both in the next week or two."

This was getting more and more bizarre.

"Week or two?" Sharpe asked, incredulous.

"Maybe. Let me ask you a question. Are you happy with your directors?"

Oh…so that's it, Greg thought. This was about one of his departmental directors.

"Mr. Patterson, let me stop you right there. I am very happy with my leaders, and I think all five of them do a great job representing our company and as an example for our employees."

"I'm glad you think so. I think so, too. Greg, I think you are a good man, with a good staff and a good group of employees."

Greg Sharpe began to rub his hands together under the table, clearly agitated.

"But you think something needs to change . . . So if it isn't me, and it isn't my people, then what is the problem?"

Mr. Patterson smiled warmly to comfort him.

"As you know, there is a lot that goes into building a strong business. And sometimes, whether it's a group of athletes, a group of salesmen, or a group of teachers, sometimes even when you have excellent ingredients, the meal doesn't turn out as well as you might have hoped.

Now, I'm not suggesting anybody should lose his job . . . but I am suggesting that if you keep doing the same things, then we'll keep getting similar results. And I expect we both want better results than what this location has been getting."

Greg didn't reply, but listened intently.

"One of the reasons I took this job is, because I believe CDI operates with a different set of values than our competitors. We are a family business who has continued to grow because of the relationships and reputation we've built in our communities. And I don't believe in dismissing someone because of mediocre sales. Those are not the results I'm most focused on."

Patterson paused, but Sharpe was stone-faced and waiting with a furrowed brow to hear the whole monologue before he responded.

"Greg, I think there's something missing in your program."

At this point, Greg Sharpe was moving from concerned confusion to restless anger.

"Really? And what do you think is missing?"

Patterson was aware of his shift in emotion, and worked to ensure that this remained a productive conversation.

"Greg, I don't want to criticize your performance. What I do want is to figure out, together, what we can do differently if we want different results. Let me ask – do you have a written strategic plan that describes what you want to accomplish and prioritize?"

Did this guy really want to question his strategy?

"Mr. President, every strategic planning instrument and tool we have implemented over the last year, or so was taken directly from research based practices that a major consulting firm has shared with at least a dozen growing Fortune 500 companies. Our X's and O's are not something…"

"Greg…" the president interrupted him, "I think you misunderstood my question."

"I think that our strategy and processes and metrics are pretty sound, Sir."

There was a definite edge and defensiveness in his voice, and Patterson recognized it.

"Greg, one thing I have learned in my time both as a coach and CEO is that culture trumps strategy. If you have a plan for what you do with your X's and O's to build your offense or defense or special teams, wouldn't you agree that you should also have a plan for building culture and team camaraderie?"

Greg rubbed his chin and listened.

"Well, I know you coached and played football before you got into business. And I would wager that you know a lot more about both football and furniture than I do. But I assure you that I am more than qualified in the area of building and improving teams. And I think that is an area where you and your staff have struggled."

"What makes you say that?"

"I know you have good intentions, but something is getting in the way of your results. This location is underperforming. And it isn't the people, or the processes, or the product, then we need to find out what else it could be that is keeping you from the growth that I think we both believe is possible here."

That last comment stung a bit. Nobody likes to hear that they are doing a poor job.

"Please don't take any of this the wrong way. I said I want to help you to find out what is missing, and I mean that. This is about admitting there is a need and then working to fill the gap to improve our company."

Greg had not expected their meeting to be anything like this.

"Mr. Patterson, I know we've plateaued a bit, and I know some of the employees may have been complaining about some of our changes. Heck, your office may have gotten a few phone calls. But I'm not sure what you're saying you want me to do."

Matthew Patterson smiled warmly. "I'm not talking about profit margins, Coach. Financials are just a symptom of the beliefs and behaviors a group has committed to . . . but as of yesterday, your program has lost two people who are transferring out of this location.

And to be honest, I just haven't seen the enthusiasm that I know is necessary to produce the success you want."

The president leaned forward, placing his weight on the forearms that rested on the table between them. "I want you to think a moment, Greg, and then answer me honestly. Do you think there is something missing . . . something you need to give more attention to?"

At first Sharpe shook his head, his pride applauding the staunch determination to hold onto his belief he had done everything he knew of to make this a great program.

And then he felt it...

It wasn't doubt. It was more like a vague awareness.

Somewhere beneath the pride and stubborn internal insistence that he and his staff had done well and worked hard and given their best, there was a tiny thought that crept up from inside him.

The thought wasn't bold or loud, but it whispered insistently to him.

It was echoing what he had said to players so often in his very brief coaching career:

If you knew better, you would do better."

He never criticized a player for not knowing something. It was his job to educate them.

And when they were taught, when they had gotten better information and techniques, they became better players. A good player – and a good coach – had to remain aware of his own need to keep improving.

"Mr. Patterson, I guess I'd be a poor coach and even worse manager if I didn't agree that everybody could learn more. And when you know better, you can do better. That is what I used to tell our guys, and it is just as true for me and my staff here."

Patterson nodded.

"As I mentioned at the start of our conversation today, I think it's my job to do everything I can to help you and your people be successful. Do you know who Jack Welch is?"

"Of course. Why?"

"Well, as the head guy at GE, Jack Welch used to go around saying 'be happy to work here, but be ready to leave.'"

Patterson paused again to let him consider the phrase.

"Now, Welch didn't say that to spread fear. He was a good leader who worked hard at developing and encouraging his people. What he meant was that he wanted everyone of his workers at GE to enjoy being there – and if they didn't, he felt that each one of them should be willing to leave and go where they would get more appreciation and development. Welch believed that was the key to keeping his managers focused on retaining and developing talent."

He stopped and waited for Greg to respond.

"Sir, I honestly don't know what you want me to change. I am always looking at improving our processes to help our people, but I can't imagine who or what convinced you that there is something wrong with what we are doing. Is it one of the people leaving who complained on their way out? Has one of the other employees said something to you?"

"You know I've been talking to company leaders at various locations the last few weeks."

"Yeah."

"Well, it was one of your directors that suggested something needed to change. I'd prefer to keep the name confidential now, as the individual requested to talk with you about it personally."

Greg felt like he had been punched in the gut. He sat quiet, without responding, for a few long moments.

"Okay. Wow." Greg's eyes remained fixed on the wood laminate floor.

"So what did you have in mind for me the next couple of weeks?"

"Well, Greg, I'm glad you asked . . . You see, when I was a coach, I liked to take my assistants on a trip to visit other programs or go to clinics to pick up new ideas in the offseason. We would use that time to evaluate the program and talk about what needed to be done."

Sharpe nodded, but had no idea how those coaching clinic trips were relevant.

"Whatever it is that's missing, you and your staff need to spend time together to work through fixing it together. But, I think that maybe you need more than a coaching conference. In fact, I'd like to pay for you and your management team to take a trip together and meet a friend of mine . . . Have you ever been rafting?"

"Rafting?"

"On a river – whitewater rapids... It's a two-day trip, maybe three depending on what you and your people decide. One of the managers that worked with the team I coached years ago has spent most every summer at one of the rafting companies on the Nantahala."

Patterson wrote a name and number on the legal pad that had sat in front of him during their conversation.

"Ask for Mitch. It'll be completely free for you and your people. Hotel too . . . Just send Ms. Cassidy the receipts."

Sharpe reached out to take the paper that the president was offering him.

"Have a great time. See if your staff can figure out what needs to change."

"Okay . . . I'll look into it."

Patterson stood up to show that the meeting was over.

"I'm glad to have you here at CDI, Greg. Let's talk next week after you get back."

Greg Sharpe stood, shook Patterson's hand a bit less firmly than he had when they had first greeted each other nearly an hour before, and walked the president to the door to end one of the most bizarre meetings he could recall.

As he backed out of his parking space to leave, Patterson yelled back from the window of his rental car: "Have a great time, Greg!"

"Yep," Greg thought to himself.

"Great."

CHAPTER 3

FINDING A GUIDE

"HONEY, I'VE GOT GOOD news and bad news."

Lisa Sharpe was not used to her husband being coy. He was direct. He was dependable. Sometimes he was even dull and predictable – but Greg Sharpe was seldom one to offer her or anyone else many conversational surprises.

"Everything okay? What happened in your meeting?"

There was more concern in her voice than she had meant for him to hear.

"Don't worry. I still have a job. So do you want the good first or the bad?"

"You know me . . . what's the good news?"

"The good news is that you don't have to put up with me leaving dirty dishes in the sink for a couple of days next week."

"What do you mean?"

"Well, I know how you enjoy cleaning up after me . . . but something else has come up."

"What something else? What are you talking about, Greg?"

"Well, baby, that's the bad news..."

"You better tell me right now what happened in that meeting!"

He chuckled a bit, first at her fretfulness and then at himself for thinking this would be an entertaining way to let her know what he and the new president had talked about.

"Baby, the bad news is that I'm going river rafting."

"You WHAT? Why? You can't swim, Greg! That's just..."

"I'll tell you all about it when I get home," he interrupted. "I'm almost to the neighborhood now."

When he pulled into the driveway, Lisa was waiting for him outside the house with hands on her hips – and a confused scowl on her face.

He hugged her and explained the strange conversation that he had with President Patterson, and did his best to answer the bombardment of questions that followed.

Mostly, he just reassured her that yes, he was still the general manager of the Nashville location . . . that no, he wasn't in any trouble . . . and that no, he didn't know what Mr. Patterson wanted him to change. But maybe, he and his management staff could get some things out in the open on this rafting trip they were supposed to take.

Eventually they went inside, but the rest of the afternoon her barrage of questions was like a bag of microwaved popcorn. After the initial and frantic popping of questions that she had shared in the driveway, there were still a few question kernels that didn't pop until later.

Over dinner, there were a couple more that popped up, and then while she was brushing her teeth there was one last burst of curiosity about the trip that she was compelled to ask him – although by that point he had tired of repeating the phrase "I don't know...," so he just twisted his hands to show her his palms and shrugged his shoulders for her instead.

Dinner turned out to be a pizza delivery (because Lisa was too consumed with interrogating her husband to cook the pork loin in the refrigerator). Afterwards, Greg called the number he had been given to schedule the river rafting trip he and his assistants would be taking together.

The woman who answered the phone was very helpful in providing information about where they were located, what the trip would consist of, and when they should arrive to check in.

When Greg mentioned he would like to schedule himself and five other adults for the following Thursday, and also would like to find a hotel nearby, she shared a number to a nearby lodge called the Freemont that offered rooms and a nice breakfast.

Greg figured they could leave sometime Wednesday morning and turn it into a nice getaway to review their plans for the upcoming year. He was bothered by the news that someone on his staff had talked to the president behind his back, though.

Greg was fairly certain it couldn't have been Walt Parker – they had been together too long for something like that to come from him. He hated not knowing which of his other four directors had torpedoed him, though.

By the time their pizza arrived, Greg had secured reservations for his staff to stay at the Freemont Inn on Wednesday evening and then to go down the river together on Thursday.

They could be home late Thursday night, and he was pretty sure the trip wouldn't be an issue for his people. They knew to set aside the week after annual reviews for late night meetings to discuss clients, marketing, and decide on strategic planning for the next four quarters.

Trisha Thomas, who led their design department, may have been the one who called Patterson. Greg knew they had butted heads a couple times about the changes he had put in place to streamline their customer experience.

He texted each of his directors that evening to meet in his office on Monday morning at 8:00 am.

That would give Trisha time to get her daughter to school, and Greg could put together an itinerary and try to explain what he and the president had discussed.

If nothing else, Sharpe thought, the rafting trip would give him a chance to find out for sure who it was that had spoken with the president and if that could get straightened out, they might have some fun doing something different together.

In spite of his past water experiences, part of him, after being on the phone organizing the trip, was looking forward to it.

Just after 9:00 pm, as Lisa was tucking in their daughter, he called his brother in law to fill him in on the day's events.

"Hi Greg! How did it go?"

Greg explained, with as much detail as he could recall, what had happened over the course of his meeting with Mr. Patterson, the Commercial Design and Corporate Interiors President.

His brother in law didn't interrupt him, except to share a few "wow's" or "hmm's" to show he was still listening.

"So what do you think he meant when he said something was missing?"

"I really don't know, man. I honestly don't know if he knows. I think this rafting thing might be like a fishing trip, where we don't know what we're supposed to catch."

"Well, it does sound fishy – I'll give you that."

"But you know what, Ben? Even though it was uncomfortable, I feel like he wants me to be there. He even said it. I really think he wants to help."

"Well, be sure you wear a life jacket. Don't want another tubing incident, right?"

There it was. The jab.

When Greg had first started dating Lisa, her brother Ben was still working as a manager at AT&T, and they had all gotten together at Lake Murray to spend the day on a boat that one of Ben's buddies owned.

Greg was so eager to impress her that he neglected to tell Lisa that he couldn't swim.

And when it came time to try tubing, he figured it would be okay – until he was flipped off the tube during a sharp turn and the fear and nervousness from his childhood short-circuited all rational thought and sent him into a frenzy of flailing arms and gasping panic.

Of course, Lisa thought it was sweet once he explained that he had never learned how to swim, but that he wanted to be with her more than he wanted to be on safe on land.

Ben, of course, didn't think it was quite as romantic.

Ben had always been one or two steps ahead in climbing the corporate success ladder, and had always seemed to hold jobs that were just a bit flashier.

Being a strategic consultant who sold advice to guys like Greg now pretty much secured Ben Cooper a superior place in the world's perception.

"Hey, just kidding Greg. Long time ago, right? So, did you have a question for me about putting together your sales quota metrics?"

"Nah – we can go over it some other time. Have a good night, Ben"

Greg Sharpe put down his phone and went upstairs to join his wife.

He was curious to see the expressions from his staff of departmental directors when he shared the news with them, and later that night had trouble sleeping as he continued to think about the trip and his location's performance and the questions that Patterson had asked him . . .

Finally, after nearly an hour of staring at the ceiling, Greg dragged himself out of bed.

When he arrived at the CDI offices the next morning, just before 7:30 am., there were already three cars in the parking lot.

Greg Sharpe pulled in beside the Ford Explorer that Walt Parker drove, and went inside. When he had made his way down the hallway and past the showroom floor of desk samples and assorted tables and chairs, he opened the door to the conference room and saw all but two of his staff already there.

The seats at the large oval wooden table that were usually filled by Trisha Thomas and Cory Ellis were empty, but would likely be occupied soon, as Cory often worked out before coming in and Trisha was probably waving goodbye to her daughter after dropping her off at school.

The conference room was not very large, but did provide enough room for the table and twelve executive chairs, a flat screen television for presentations mounted on the far wall, and a long wall of shelves opposite the door.

Susan White was a petite woman in her mid-fifties, and had been part of CDI for almost fifteen years, working as their director of the design department for the last six. She had seen the Nashville location grow from barely ten million to over forty million in sales, and her critical eye and strong personality were disguised by a very polite demeanor.

Susan was sitting with her back to the door. Greg recognized her black ponytail, which moved slightly as she nodded across the table in a conversation with Andy.

Andy Butler was a younger guy, and Susan's opposite in a number of ways. Andy was married, was in his early thirties, and was completely bald. He was far more emotional and charismatic as well, and those traits had served him well as the director of sales.

The third person at the table was Walt Parker, who was sitting beside Andy.

Walt and Greg had been friends for years, and when Greg was offered the job as GM of the CDI Nashville location, Walt was the second person he called.

Having worked well together at their last company, Greg was thrilled to have Walt agree to join him in making the move to CDI – and was even happier to be able to promote him to director of inventory a few months earlier.

Walt made the move easier for both of them, and his greying goatee always seemed to frame a warm smile, even when Greg or one of their coworkers felt overwhelmed by the day's issues.

All the three, who had been talking quietly amongst themselves at the conference table, sprang up excitedly from their chairs when their general manager walked in.

The first question Greg heard was from Andy Butler. "So, do we all still work here?"

Greg sighed and gave them an exasperated grin. "Yep... We still work here."

He only peeked inside the door, though, and said,

"Let me know when the other two show up – I want to talk to everybody at the same time."

He checked both his personal and his business email twice and surfed the web impatiently waiting for Trisha and Cory to arrive.

Twenty uncomfortable minutes later, Sharpe saw his other two directors walk in.

Greg Sharpe emerged from his office and motioned for everyone to sit down together.

Part of him wanted to open up and tell his staff everything about his conversation with President Patterson, while another part of him was still seething with anger that one of these five people would go behind his back and question his leadership.

When everyone was seated and looking at him with quiet anticipation, Sharpe took a deep breath and spoke.

"Okay, so I'm sure you are wondering why I asked you all to meet me here early today. The short version is that we've been asked to take a trip."

The conversation about their upcoming trip wasn't a long one.

After giving a short description of his meeting with Patterson and outlining when he hoped they could leave, when they were tentatively returning, and what they would each probably need to bring, Sharpe gave them the rest of the morning to confirm that they could arrange their lives to accommodate the trip.

By 11:00 am he had heard from each of them that, while it was unexpected and a bit of an inconvenience, they would be able to make it work. Trisha was able to get her mother to stay at the house with Lucy, and the others were able to make similar arrangements where needed.

Most of them even mentioned they thought the trip sounded like fun.

When Wednesday arrived, Sharpe and his management staff took care of as much office work as they could prior to lunchtime, and then left the CDI parking lot together in the Chevy Tahoe that Greg's wife usually drove. His truck didn't have enough room for all six passengers and their luggage.

The rafting trip would take just under two days, bringing them home Thursday night.

Driving from Nashville to Bryson, North Carolina would take around five hours.

All six of them were able to sit comfortably in the vehicle, and they made only one stop before dinner time, so Greg could get more gas and give them all a chance to grab a snack or get out and stretch their legs a bit.

There was little conversation that afternoon on the road together, and there was an odd sense of discomfort that no one acknowledged – but that Greg certainly felt – even after they arrived at a restaurant for dinner.

Dinner passed with a series of shallow conversations and friendly jabs as they joked with each other and talked. Everyone avoided the topic of what was missing or what was going to happen, when they arrived at the rafting company the next day.

They finished dinner and soon made it to the hotel, where they said good night and settled into their rooms to watch television and to call home.

The next morning, after filling themselves with a nice buffet breakfast, the CDI management team were loaded up and finally on their way to go rafting.

It was still before lunch time when Greg pulled off of Highway 74 into the gravel parking lot where the Googled directions had led them.

The rafting company was little more than a collection of three old wooden buildings.

Sharpe turned off the engine. "Here we are, guys."

There were a few other cars in the gravel lot beside them, and Sharpe got out and began walking toward the main building, where a sign invited visitors to register.

There were a couple of mobile home trailers, all shaded by tall pine trees, and a half dozen picnic tables with benches in an open area near the river to their left.

The group walked past a large open barn where paddles, kayaks, rafts, and life vests waited to be rented. All five of the directors followed him, and they each peeked at the river as they walked toward the main building that housed a small collection of t-shirts, souvenirs, and a cash register.

The place apparently used college-aged kids as guides and workers, and Sharpe smiled as he approached a guy with long blonde hair pulled back into a pony tail that was waiting behind the counter to greet customers.

"Hi – I'm Greg Sharpe. My staff and I have a reservation with Mitch today. Is that you?"

The long haired guy chuckled.

"No, sir. I'm Eddie."

Eddie brushed a renegade hair out of his face and looked down at his clipboard, then took a pen from the counter to write something on the paper it held.

"I got you guys checked in. Looks like everything's paid for already, so you're good to go. Mitch should be here in a few minutes to take you to the barn and grab your stuff."

Greg thanked him, and turned to the others there with him in the makeshift gift shop.

"See anything you can't live without?"

Andy Butler was adjusting an orange baseball cap that he had grabbed from one of the shelves.

"Maybe. I don't want my brains to get cooked." He rubbed his bald head, slipped the cap on, and then leaned over to look at himself in a small mirror hanging on the wall.

"It's definitely you, Andy," Walt laughed. "Better keep that thing covered up. We bald men need protection!"

Walt Parker patted his own hat as he spoke.

He was wearing the same floppy weathered tan Aussie-style hat that he had worn at every company outing Andy could remember since they had met.

Greg had no hat, and didn't intend to purchase one. He had sunglasses tethered to his neck – and that would be the extent of his accessories for the afternoon.

Looking at his staff, though, Greg couldn't help, but laugh as he considered the motley bunch of personalities he had brought to the river. CDI had five very capable and interesting directors, and they were each an important part of the growth Greg hoped to accomplish.

Walt Parker rubbed his greying goatee and looked around the store at the collection of shirts and rafting merchandise. He was Greg's closest friend on the staff, and had come to CDI with him less than two years ago. The hair on his chin had become a bit greyer now that Walt had reached his forties. Parker was steady and calming voice, and helped Greg by never getting too high or too low in the middle of any triumph or tragedy.

Tricia Thomas, the director of operations, was still in her late thirties and had been divorced for a few years now. She had one daughter, Lucy, who was the center of her universe.

Tricia was perfect in her role as their Director of Operations, because she was a stickler about minutiae – and even in this casual setting, her flawlessly styled short brown hair demonstrated her attention to detail.

Greg leaned toward believing it was her that had secretly spoken to Patterson.

He watched as Tricia walked over to Walt Parker and jokingly handed him a pair of gaudy pink sunglasses from off one of the racks. Parker laughed with her, tried them on and posed a moment, then put the glasses back on the rack, before they moved toward to door talking and laughing together.

Andy Butler continued to adjust his new baseball cap after he had paid for it.

Andy was a young guy – still in his late twenties – and was the CDI director of sales. He was a graduate of UT, and had that alma mater in common with Susan White.

Susan was content to watch the others, and her calm brown eyes quietly observed the rest of the group and their activity. Susan didn't speak much, but when she did it was normally important and insightful. She definitely had a designer's discerning disposition.

Outside the registration and souvenir building, Cory Ellis was on his phone. He was Director of Installations and even in his mid-thirties was still in good enough shape to lift and carry heavy pieces as well as any of the men who worked in his department.

Happily single and in his early thirties, Ellis worked hard to stay in better shape than his peers, and often worked out or played basketball in the mornings before coming in to work.

Cory was a smarter guy than most people realized, having earned a bachelor's degree in philosophy instead of business at Sewanee, a small division three school just north of Chattanooga. He was wearing a purple Sewanee Tigers t-shirt and cargo shorts.

As Greg watched through the window, Ellis put away his phone and smiled at a girl with short red hair who walked past him toward the registration building.

The girl was in her twenties, carrying a red backpack on one shoulder, and she peeked her head into the registration building to ask if they were waiting on a rafting guide.

"We're waiting for Mitch." Greg said. "He's supposed to take us down the river today."

She asked, "Is that who Patterson said to ask for?" and motioned for him and his staff to join her outside.

Greg spoke up. "Yes, ma'am. He said to ask specifically for Mitch."

"Well, that doesn't surprise me. But I gave up that nickname years ago."

Sharpe was confused.

"Sophia Mitchell." She held out her hand. "I'll be your guide today, Mister Sharpe."

His assistants broke into laughter.

"So this is Mitch?" Ellis asked, amused.

"Wow. I'm sorry." Greg stammered, "I just thought…"

"It's okay. I'm sure Coach Patterson is having a nice laugh in his office right now. He used to call me Mitch when I was his team manager." Sophia put down her backpack and shook hands with each of the members of the group as she spoke.

Sophia said, "it took less time than yelling my whole name. But I had a great time working with him."

Greg nodded, unsure what their next step was.

"And I was excited to hear he was sending another group to raft with me."

"So we aren't the first group Patterson has referred to you?" Andy asked.

"Oh, yeah… First group from his new job, I guess."

Sophia grabbed her bag and walked them past the clearing where the picnic tables were. The river was on their right, and it stretched nearly forty yards wide, mumbling incomprehensibly as it rolled against the rocky shore.

"He's asked me to guide lots of people over the last few years," she continued. "You guys are a furniture company, right?"

"Yes ma'am" Tricia said.

Sophia continued to walk, leading them to a smaller building hidden off near the edge of the grounds. The building was not very large – maybe twenty-feet long on each side, and had been painted dark green a long time ago. On the door was a sign that said "Conference Room."

"This is where we're going to start."

She opened the door, flipped on a switch, and pointed to the two long tables inside.

There were folding chairs leaning in a stack against the wall, so Greg and his staff each grabbed a chair and then all sat down together around one of the tables. Andy grabbed an extra chair for Sophia, who placed her backpack on the other table and sat down with the group that had hired her to be their river guide.

"Okay, ladies and gents. I'll get you to the equipment barn and go over our rules for the river in a little while. But first, I want to be sure we're on the same page about why you are spending the day with me today."

Greg looked at his watch. It was almost 11:30. But before he could speak, one of his assistants replied.

"To hold hands and sing songs with each other?" Cory joked, his voice laced with more than a hint of cynicism.

Andy snickered, and Greg sighed.

Sophia nodded without judgment. "Really?"

"Sophia, we honestly don't know," Greg interjected. "My new boss, your old coach, thinks there's something we aren't doing well as a staff. That's why we're here."

Sophia nodded.

"Hmmm. So have you and your staff talked about what the problem might be?"

Six intelligent people cast their eyes at the table or floor, unresponsive.

Greg answered after a few moments had passed. "We haven't talked about it a lot as a staff . . . but I'm not really sure there is a problem."

Sophia nodded again and looked around. "So, you guys feel like everything is going well in your organization as it should?"

She saw a couple of men shrugging their shoulders. Greg looked around anxiously, curious to hear their response.

Sophia allowed the room to remain silent for a few uncomfortable seconds.

Finally, Walt Parker spoke up.

"Yeah. I'll say it." He looked directly at Sophia. "I think we could do some things better."

Greg turned and stared with surprise at his longtime friend and coworker.

Sophia nodded again.

"Okay."

She went to the other table where her red backpack was resting, and reached inside to pull out a stack of index cards.

"That your bag of tricks?" asked Greg.

"Something like that. More like my tool box." She gave each of the group members a few index cards, and then reached inside one of the front pockets to provide a pen for them to use.

Greg and his staff waited to hear what she had planned for them.

"Let me start by saying this . . . You are like most of the groups that I have guided before you, and probably not any different from the many that I will guide in the future. It doesn't matter that furniture is your focus.

"You are working with a group of people who are struggling to implement the ideas in your playbook. That isn't just a sports problem or a furniture problem. That is an *every industry problem*.

Every one of the groups I've guided over the last couple of years has a similar story. Whether they are dentists, or teachers, or salesmen, or athletes, or widget makers, most problems that management groups experience are the result of placing too much focus on developing their playbook, and not enough focus on developing their people.

Think about it this way. Imagine your College President, back when he was just a basketball coach, had spent hours on drawing up plays, and put together the best playbook in the entire state. No matter how great the plays were, if he didn't have players with talent, or if those players didn't work well together, the playbook would have looked like a disaster to anybody watching his team from the stands.

The reality is that you guys are just like the IT group I had in last week and the group of teachers that are scheduled to come in tomorrow. You need to develop relationships and roles for the people who you plan to trust with your playbook. Putting together a playbook is much easier than bringing together a team of people who will execute it.

It's the soft stuff that is always really the hard stuff.

That is why you guys are here. And my job is to guide you through the same team development process that you will be able to replicate with your people back at your office."

She paused to take a breath while Greg and the five departmental directors quietly considered what she had said. Most of them seemed impressed, but Greg was reserving his judgment.

"Now, before we do anything else today, I want to walk you through a quick activity that will make our time on the water a lot more valuable."

Greg and Cory Ellis shared a glance and roll their eyes, and then Greg mumbled one word quietly to himself as she began giving directions.

"Great."

CHAPTER 4

THE PROBLEM

"SO," SOPHIA CONTINUED, "ON the table in front of you, each person should have a handful of index cards and a pen."

The group of directors looked around the table at each other, exchanging curious looks of uncertainty.

"Here is what I want you to do. Take your pens and number from one to three, skipping a line in between each to give room for your responses."

She paused briefly to give them time, surveying their behavior.

"Now, this will only be useful, if you are honest and take it seriously. Can I trust you to do that?"

Everyone nodded their agreement.

"Okay, then. Think before you write anything. Ready?"

"Yes, ma'am," said Walt Parker, somewhat impatiently.

"Good. Okay, I want you to imagine that everyone in your company, after drinking from the same water supply, has fallen ill. On your index cards, I want you to write down your answers to three questions. Number one, what would you name the illness..."

Cory Ellis placed his hands on the table, leaned back, and shook his head.

Greg, wrinkling his brow, nodded for Cory to write. The other four were already leaning over their cards, with pens moving.

"For number two, identify who it was that drugged the water."

Sophia paused again, watching them all think and write.

When everyone had paused and was waiting for her next direction, she continued...

"And for number three, what is the antidote?"

Susan White was the first to finish and put her pen down, but within only a couple of minutes all of the others had stopped writing.

Sophia walked around the table and collected their cards, then stood in front of them at the end of the table. "Any idea why we started with this?" she asked.

They didn't answer, but she waited patiently for someone to speak up.

Andy Butler adjusted his new hat and looked down at the table.

Cory, a moment later, mumbled another attempt at humor: "to make sure we don't drink too much?"

Sophia grinned. "Anyone else?"

"Cause we need to fix what's broken," Walt said, boldly.

Greg Sharpe was startled, surprised again by his friend's firm reply.

Sophia nodded at him, gratefully.

"Yes, Mister, uh – "

"Parker"

"Thank you. Mister Parker is right." Sophia began to walk around the table, focusing on each person in turn as she talked. "The worst problem ANY team can have is to not admit that it has problems . . . Each of you is a leader, right?"

Everyone in the group nodded.

"So what is the most important trait that a leader should have?"

"Do we need to write this down?" Greg asked.

"Nope. Just asking. Any ideas?"

Cory Ellis spoke up. "Integrity."

"That's a good one" Sophia affirmed.

"Discipline. Work ethic." Greg said.

Andy Butler looked to Tricia, beside him, whose hand was raised.

"I think leaders have to be Knowledgeable," she said. "They have to have enough experience to know what they are talking about and asking others to do."

Susan White nodded agreement. "Yeah . . . I like that, Tricia. Competent."

"Trust. They have to be willing to trust their people," Parker added.

He looked directly at Greg, then down at the floor.

"You gotta motivate," Butler said. "Have to have intensity. Passionate, I guess."

"Those are all very important, but I think they are secondary traits," Sophia explained.

Greg and his staff waited to hear her suggestion.

"Years ago, Coach Patterson and I were talking about one of the backup point guards. He had a good work ethic, knew the game, had experience, played with intensity, but he seemed to put himself in a lot of bad situations..."

She looked at Walt, as she continued.

"And I think he trusted his teammates, too. But he lacked something that every great leader has to have..."

She paused for effect.

"The most important trait for leaders is awareness. Without that, the others are useless..."

She made her way over to the wall, grabbed a blue marker from the tray beneath a whiteboard, and drew a three column chart.

On the far left column, she began to write their answers to the first question.

"Tolstoy wrote that 'Happy families are all alike; but every unhappy family is unhappy in its own way.'"

While she spoke, Greg and his staff read the names for their imagined team illnesses, as she wrote them in capital blue letters on the board.

UNCONNECTEDITIS
BLAME SYNDROME
NEGATIVISM
IRON ALLERGIES
CLIQUE-N-POX
THE COMMON COLD

She finished writing and turned to the group of coaches. "These six illnesses are what you wrote down that are making your family unhappy. They describe what your team might be suffering from . . . and I think they are all important to discuss."

She stopped and stood behind Greg.

"They are all symptoms that you have seen somewhere in your organization – and they are actually many of the same symptoms that the leaders in lots of other organizations experience. You aren't alone – there are managers and administrators and coaches and supervisors in virtually any industry you can imagine that have these same issues. Identifying symptoms is important as evidence that something is wrong. Remember, great leadership begins with awareness."

She pointed to the whiteboard.

"Which of you wrote 'unconnected-itis?'"

Cory Ellis raised his right hand up just above his brow.

"That'd be me."

"Okay. And you are…?"

"Cory. Coach Ellis."

"Thanks, Cory. What did you mean when you wrote that?"

He looked at Greg and then rubbed his goatee before speaking. "I meant that we call ourselves a family, but we really don't feel like one. We don't feel like a real team. We aren't nearly as close as I was with teammates when I was a player. I think that's part of the reason a couple of our people are thinking of leaving."

Sophia nodded, and scanned the rest of the staff.

"Does anyone else feel like that?"

"I guess I do…" Butler answered. "I'm the one that wrote 'clique-n-pox.'"

Everyone waited for him to continue.

"Well, what I meant was that we have guys, like Cory said, who don't know each other or what their story is. We have sales, design and inventory, but even in my department, it seems like the people don't spend time with other departments. We're all split up into cliques."

He looked around at his coworkers, and turned his palms up asking for their agreement.

All but Greg seemed to nod their consensus.

"Well, all I see wrong right now with our guys is a good, old-fashioned case of finger pointing and blaming others for mistakes, Greg said. "Blame syndrome was mine."

He looked first at Sophia, and then to Walt, to make his point.

"Cliques don't matter to me. Just be where you're supposed to be and do your job the right way. Right Walt? What was yours, anyway?"

Walt hesitated a moment, and in the silence Tricia decided to offer her two cents.

"I wrote the negativism," she said. "We look like kicked dogs sometimes. There's no positive fire or enthusiasm. And, even when a person does something good to help out or lands a big account, we just move on."

She avoided Greg's eyes, and spoke to Sophia.

"The team just seems more down than they should."

"That's great so far, everybody," she replied. She looked to Walt and Susan White, who had not yet spoken.

"Would you two like to share your ideas?"

"Okay." Susan White sat up and adjusted herself in the chair.

She was an attractive older woman with a small frame, and the chair seemed too large for her.

"I'll share mine." She looked at Cory. "You know how hard you and your crew work when you are running overtime with installations?"

Ellis nodded slightly.

"Well sir, I don't know that we have five people on staff inside the building that put in the work you do. They show up five times a week, and they know how to look busy, but when I watch them, a good bit of our productivity is lost, because they just go through the motions. Iron Allergies was mine. I just don't think we have people invested enough to do the heavy lifting or take the initiative they should, to tell the truth."

Greg seemed to take that personally, and wrinkled his forehead as he listened.

Then he turned to Walt.

"So I guess you wrote down the common cold?"

Parker nodded. "Yep."

"See, at least you and me are on the same page. Things really aren't that bad!"

Parker frowned and turned his chin to one side, and measured his words before speaking.

Greg and his staff all waited for Parker's answer.

"Greg, I want to be on the same page with you. We go back more than a few years together, and I think you are a good man."

He turned his body to speak directly to his friend.

"You know me, Greg. I always thought common was just about the worst thing you could be. Common doesn't require much work. Or much passion. Common is just ordinary. And ordinary gets forgotten. Ordinary gets fired, Greg."

He took a deep breath.

"The common cold – that is exactly what's wrong with our company. With us, even. You want to implement new strategies and think they're gonna make it better. But, one more policy ain't gonna change that chilly feeling in our offices. And I know that, by themselves, your brother-in-law's consulting ideas aren't gonna make us less common."

Greg took the comments like punches in his gut. But Parker wasn't through talking.

"Greg, man, I didn't know that Patterson would send us rafting – but I did meet with him last week. Just before you did. And it's probably my fault he told you that we needed to do something different."

Greg's mouth fell open, and his shoulders drooped in disbelief.

"You?"

Parker closed his eyes and nodded.

When he opened them again to explain, Greg had gotten up from his chair.

His most loyal employee, the one he counted as his closest friend, was the man who had gone and torpedoed him with the CDI President?

"We ARE missing something." Walt continued. "And just going through the motions of changing our strategy isn't what we need. We need something else. Maybe we'll get it here – I don't know, but Mitch is right. We got issues, man."

Greg stood frozen in shock, and sighed.

He shook his head, and then surprised himself with a burst of anger. "That's Crazy!"

Without saying another word, he turned to open the door and went outside. He didn't go far, but he needed a moment to collect himself.

After a letting out two long, controlled breaths, Greg gathered himself and realized he needed to return. When he walked back inside, his people were still at the table, and Sophia was writing down their answers to the second question on the whiteboard.

"Sorry, guys." Greg said, as he sat back down. "I do want us to get better. Makes no sense for me to argue with what you guys are seeing."

He reached over to put his hand on Walt's shoulder.

"If you say we need to do something different . . . I trust you."

Greg turned to Sophia. "So what's next, Miss Mitchell?"

She pointed at the whiteboard.

"When he was coaching, Patterson used to tell our players never to just point at a problem."

She motioned to the left side of the chart, where she had written the list of illnesses they had each described.

"He said that 'pointers were usually part of the problem.' A good teammate's was supposed to make things better by suggesting a solution. Awareness is about acknowledging realities and talking about the elephant in the room..."

She motioned to the middle column now. "But effective leadership is about more than just an awareness . . . it's about getting past the symptom and finding the cause, and then taking action to address it and tame the elephant."

She smiled at Greg.

"So here are the answers to your second question, about who drugged the water."

On the board were their six responses.

UNDERACHIEVERS
SHARPE
US
TEAM LEADERS
ME
MANAGERS

"Anybody see a pattern up there?" she asked.

"Looks like I'm the only one who is worried about people being responsible for meeting their numbers." Greg said, looking around. "Underachievers blame everybody, but themselves."

He heard himself and the words coming out of his mouth, and slowly realized that perhaps he had been more blind than he wanted to admit.

"Yeah, well, I'll go next," said Cory. "I wrote team leaders. When I was playing ball, it was their job to control the locker room."

Sophia asked him, "What do you mean by that?"

"I mean, the best players had to get themselves

motivated. Their job as team leaders was to get everybody together."

"And if the players didn't, then what would have happened?"

"Then the coaches would've found new players. Point blank."

She paused.

"So, Cory, I'm curious. If you were given a job where you couldn't replace your players, who would be responsible for the locker room?"

He sat thinking, but didn't answer her.

"Alright, gentlemen, who else would like to share their thoughts?"

Parker's hand went up, but he didn't wait for her to invite his comment.

"I'm the one that wrote down your name, Greg. And I'm willing to take just as much blame myself – but we always said that everything starts at the top. If we are going to change the company culture, it starts with you. You gotta focus on more than just new policies and performance numbers."

Greg was less surprised than he was confused now.

Hadn't he done a good job?

Hadn't he insisted on doing things the right way?

"I just don't understand what you have a problem with, Walt. You said yourself that the processes we put in place were better than what we found when we got here...?"

"It's not the processes or policies." Susan White interrupted. Her calm voice was low, but clear. "I wrote down managers on my card. WE drugged the water. All of us. Low expectations. Work ethic. Even negativity."

She looked at Walt, then said, "We all set the tone."

Sophia stood back and let them talk to each other without interrupting.

Walt finished Susan's thought. "And that is what I'm saying. It's not about strategy. Strategy don't matter if the feeling in the office ain't right."

Tricia Thomas pointed four fingers at her own sternum.

"I wrote that it was me. If we need to be more enthusiastic and positive, I need to bring more energy."

"Us." Andy Butler took off his new orange cap and made a wide circle with it as he held it in his hand, referring to the entire staff.

"I wrote it was us. Just like Susan." He pointed his hat at Sophia before putting it on as he finished talking. "That's the pattern. Most of us agree on who's responsible."

"And that starts with me," Greg offered. "So what do we do, now?"

Sophia smiled broadly.

"Well, I'm glad you asked!" She walked back to the whiteboard.

"Symptoms are easy to treat. You can get a Kleenex for a runny nose, or watery eyes. But the Kleenex doesn't cure you."

She began to write down the last column of words from the six index cards.

"The cure comes from identifying what you were allergic to and removing it. Your organization has probably spent a lot of time and money on runny noses and watery eyes. Maybe, the symptoms you saw were negativity, or excuses and blaming, or cliques, but the key to getting healthy is to treat the cause, not just the symptom."

When she finished talking, she moved to the side of the whiteboard to let them view the final column of their answers. The six suggested antidotes they had suggested were:

REMEMBER WHY
HAVE MORE FUN
NO EXCUSES
PERFORMANCE POSTERS
SUNDAY COOKOUTS
ADD MORE EGGS

"Anybody want to go first?" Sophia asked.

"Sure," Walt offered. "I wrote that we need to remember why."

He looked at Greg and continued. "Somewhere along the way we both forgot. Remember, when we used numbers and metrics as a way to motivate and develop people? We've been more focused lately on the results instead of the people . . . Numbers are important, but they ain't why I'm here."

Greg digested the words quietly, breathing slowly and squeezing his hands together as he considered his friend's comments.

"My antidote was to have more fun," Tricia said.

"If we're being negative, or not recognizing positives, that rubs off on our employees. If we want to get them more excited, we need to reward them for successes. Find a way to make parts of our meetings fun somehow."

Sophia nodded in agreement to validate her suggestion.

"Yeah, mine was sorta like Tricia's..." Butler raised his hand as he spoke. "I wrote down the Sunday cookouts."

"I just remember how much it meant to me when I started working with you guys to have that cookout at Sharpe's house to get to know everybody. Maybe we need to do stuff like that with the rest of the company more. I think that would help with the little cliques, at least. Put them at different tables to make sure they get to know other people and other departments. I don't know . . . it's just an idea."

Greg shrugged his shoulders. "Maybe, Andy. I don't guess it would hurt."

"I had the posters." Susan's sweet, demure voice called out, and everyone turned to listen to her explain the performance posters phrase.

"I think we might benefit from placing names next to what is getting done well. Let everyone see what we expect from them and see where they are."

"In the break room?" asked Walt.

"Everywhere. Break room. Hallways. Warehouse. I believe it could motivate all of us to work harder. It could certainly create a sense of accountability."

She leaned back in her chair and placed her hands in her lap.

"No excuses..." Greg said.

"I suppose, in a way…" Susan replied.

"No – that was my antidote comment," Greg explained. "No excuses. And I was thinking about how people get defensive and point at others or at the economy when they don't meet expectations. But, now I'm thinking that it refers more to me. To us."

"So that just leaves you, Ellis. What did you mean with the eggs?" asked Walt.

Cory Ellis smiled and leaned forward, placing his forearms on the table.

"You guys ever make a cake?"

They laughed.

"Some cake mixes you buy in the store, they have powdered eggs already included in the bag, so that all you have to do is add some water."

Sophia was listening as closely as the others, curious to know where Ellis was going with his explanation.

"But if you look at Duncan Hines mixes, they're different. Do you know why Duncan Hines makes people add eggs, instead of including powdered eggs in the bag of mix?"

He sat up, taller, to deliver the answer.

"They want you own it. If all you have to do is add water, you're not really baking. Adding the eggs makes you feel more invested. Adding the eggs makes you more proud of the cake."

His eyes turned to Greg and Walt, sitting next to him.

"Our people aren't being asked to add enough eggs to the mix, Greg."

Sophia smiled.

This was perfect.

"You people are a good group. Every one of you is right."

She pointed to the three columns of phrases that were written on the whiteboard.

"Everything you mentioned is dead on. Every comment describes part of the elephant in the room. But the elephant isn't just one of them. They are all connected."

She drew a circle around the far right column of suggested antidotes, then snapped the top on the whiteboard marker and placed it in the holder on the board.

"What your team is missing -" she pointed at the board for emphasis – "is teamwork. That is what we will be learning about when we get on the water..."

She walked over to stand behind Greg and continued.

"Do you know what teamwork is?"

She waited only a moment, then gave the answer.

"According to Mr. Patterson, teamwork is the '**coordinated activities of a cohesive group contributing diverse skills and resources to accomplish a compelling common goal**.' He said, it was true for athletes or architects or anything else and more than metrics or any business strategy, it is the sense of purpose and togetherness that makes teams truly great."

Sophia paused, as she moved to grab her backpack and slid it over her right shoulder.

"When we get out on the rapids, I plan to help you with understanding and applying each part of that definition – and how to build your people into a GREAT team. But, the first team you have to build is this one."

She pointed at each of them individually.

"You have to build a strong leadership team first. So let's go get you some gear and get started on our trip down the river. That is where you are going to learn to be great."

When she walked out of the meeting room, they followed her.

Greg sighed heavily, still unsure what the day would turn into, and mumbled to himself . . .

"Great."

CHAPTER 5

GOALS and GEAR

"PUT ON A VEST and make sure to buckle it so you know it fits. Then grab a paddle and go have a seat at one of the picnic tables over there..."

Sophia was standing just outside the large equipment barn, and motioned with her hand to where the vests were hanging, then to where the paddles were collected in open barrels, and then finished by pointing to the picnic tables that were in a clearing down near the river.

Greg and his staff followed her directions, taking a moment to try on their vests before walking over to one of the tables.

The sun was bright and warm.

Cory's purple t-shirt looked almost black under the light blue life vest.

Tricia dutifully adjusted and maintained her hair in the soft wind, and Andy smiled as he proudly adjusted the orange baseball cap he had bought earlier.

When they were all seated and waiting, Sophia walked over to begin their training.

"Okay, first things first. Safety…"

She held out a paddle to illustrate.

"This is a paddle. Keep your hand on here to grip the oar, like this," and she put the plastic end of the oar in one hand, with her other firmly gripping the shaft. "Lose hold of the oar, and you will get summer tooth syndrome…"

She waited for the confused looks to arrive, and then continued…

"You know, where summer in your mouth, summer in the river, and summer in the raft!"

They all laughed with her.

"Also, that life vest you grabbed stays on and buckled at all times. Like a good teammate, its job is to lift you up when things get rough. Be glad it's there for you."

She took a breath, and then pointed at herself.

"And last, listen to your guide. You hired a guide, because you wanted someone who has been down the river before and knows about the areas that are dangerous and how to navigate them. Good guides know how to steer the raft away from trouble . . . but a guide is only as good as her crew. I need my rowers to pay attention and follow directions. You have to trust me."

She looked at them as she paused to let that last bit of instructions sink in.

"If you don't row when I ask you to, or how I ask you to, it will be more frustrating for all of us . . . and will result in your group having a much tougher day. Without a guide – or without listening to your guide, you will bump into branches or get stuck on rocks that more coachable rafters will be able to avoid."

"So, you're going to coach us?" Tricia asked.

Sophia turned to give her more of an answer than she expected.

"Whether you have been rafting before or not," she said, "I know you haven't been on the water learning from me. Think about it this way... Just because a kid goes out and runs around and around on a basketball court for a few hours doesn't mean he's gotten better or learned anything."

She moved her index in a circle for emphasis, and then continued.

"The learning comes from having a guide there to share information and teach fundamentals that the kid can use to get better. Just going out on the water together won't make you a better team. Being in the same boat doesn't make you a team, just like wearing the same uniform does not make you a team . . . am I right?"

"Right," Walt spoke up.

"Well, we're going to use this trip down the river to help you guys be a better team. This river is good for teaching people to work together. It is a fun way to teach teamwork."

"Sounds good. I'm ready to get started," Cory said impatiently.

Sophia, glad that he had opened the door for her next request, turned to face him.

"Okay, Cory . . . how about you go over there and pick a raft, then place it on the trailer?"

She pointed to a stack of rafts on the side of the equipment barn. Not too far away, on a gravel drive that wove through the property, was trailer that had a few rafts already loaded, attached to an old and dented white 15 passenger van.

"Yes, ma'am."

He jumped up and ran over to the stack of rafts, ready to show off and then paused when he pulled on the top one, and found how heavy and unwieldy it was.

After a few unsuccessful attempts to pick it up alone, with his coaching peers snickering from the picnic table as they watched him, Cory Ellis walked back over shaking his head.

"Can't do it, Sophia. I need some help if you want that raft lifted."

Sophia grinned at him.

"Perfect. That's our first lesson of the day. You cannot do anything worthwhile all by yourself. No matter how hard you try, working alone is less effective – and a lot less fun."

Everyone in the group listened as Sophia made her point.

"Too many people want to do it all by themselves. Teamwork is about asking for help and making more and better things possible! Even something that seems as simple as carrying a raft. How about all six of you try it together this time?"

Greg nodded and got up, and his staff followed his lead.

All six of them walked over to where the stack of rafts were sitting, and each person grabbed a part of it with his hand.

With all six people involved, lifting it was easy.

Then they pulled against one another without making much progress for a moment until Walt said, "This way . . . we'll go load it on the trailer over there."

He pointed to an open spot on the trailer rack, and without another word they placed it there and returned to the picnic table where Sophia was waiting.

"Perfect. So, you came here with the first part of building a team already taken care of. The first part – a very important one – is choosing who is going to get into the boat with you. But once your team has been chosen, there are five steps to becoming a GREAT team. The first one is identifying your goals and making sure you have the gear you will need."

She held up her index finger.

"Goals and gear are the first part of the team building process. Without them, the rest would just be overlooked. This is the part where you make sure that everybody on the boat has what they need and is crystal clear about why they are there."

She looked at Walt. "Mister Parker, this is about what you mentioned. The 'common cold' that you described is a symptom of not having a compelling common goal. Every GREAT team has a clear and inspiring goal that explains why they are there to work together. If you don't know why you are doing it, you probably won't work hard while you are doing it."

Susan White nodded at that comment. "I like that, Sophia."

"Thank you, Miss White," she smiled, "That is why I am here. See, if you were just here for fun, or just to spend some time on the water and enjoy the scenery, then you wouldn't need me as your guide. But, because I AM your guide, I will tell you that we have no reason to get in that van and drive up to put the raft in the water, if your group isn't completely clear about why we are doing it."

The six of them sat quietly, each listening intently as she spoke. Sophia was far more bold and charismatic than they had first assumed.

"And that would be?" she asked.

"The elephant," said Cory.

"Teamwork," said Greg. "If that is truly what we're missing. Either way, I'm willing to trust you as our guide to get us down the river."

"Good," Walt Parker said, almost inaudibly.

"Great," said Sophia. "But first I want to talk to you about gear."

She reached out and patted Greg's life vest, then pointed to the raft.

"Gear is important – and there is definitely a need for it. The right tools make any job easier. Gear is the stuff you need to accomplish your goals. That raft is something we need... we couldn't get down the river without it. Those vests are something you need. In your line of work, there are certain things you need, too, right?"

"Yeah, sure... trucks, phones, desks, samples..." said Sharpe.

"A computer" Cory added.

"Right," Sophia nodded. "But, I bet there is also a bunch of stuff that your company has paid for that you don't really need."

"What do you mean?" Parker asked.

"Well, our rafts are sturdy, but they aren't the nicest ones you could buy. And over there – the registration building." She pointed. "It isn't the Taj Mahal. Some people may arrive here and want it to be, but it doesn't need to be. I think that most wants just higher quality needs. And while every team needs gear, I think sometimes it can get in the way of what's important."

The group just listened as she continued.

"Let me ask you this. Has anyone on your team ever complained about gear? The quality of your office supplies? How big the building is? How new the desks are?"

"Sure, a few people will complain about things like that," said Susan.

"Then I would argue that they aren't focused on the right things. As leaders, you have to be sure that your people are safe and have the equipment they need to do their job. But you also have to be sure that they don't allow a desire for luxury to interfere with their focus. Here's the thing you need to ask . . . Is the gear that they want a distraction from their goals?"

Sophia paused to let them think.

"Gear is the necessary stuff. And better tools can help your people to get better results. But, poor leaders sometimes just throw money at a problem and think that is the solution. They get away from emphasizing the goals – and problems are solved with focus more than funding."

She looked at Greg. "You may need supplies and samples and trucks, but you also probably spent thousands on things that aren't necessary. Your people may want cool new gadgets – but those things don't win accounts for you. Thinking too much about gear can distract you from the most important thing your people need – a compelling goal. And, what if you spend your time and money on aren't moving you closer to that goal, then you may be wasting them both."

Walt nodded in agreement.

But Greg looked unsure. "So you're saying we shouldn't give our people nice stuff? That we would be a better team, if we didn't have a nice building or break room?"

Before Sophia could respond, Andy Butler spoke up.

"You know, we do have nice gear – Greg has made sure our facilities are nice. I think that shows we care about our image."

Susan White interjected, "But that stuff might have made it easier for us to get comfortable."

"Comfort without commitment produces complacency," Sophia said.

"What does that mean?" Greg asked.

"It means we have told them we want to grow and be more profitable, which are good things," said Parker. "But we also spent more time selling management on renovations than we did selling our people a compelling goal that keeps them up at night or gets them up every morning hungry to win those accounts."

"I'm not saying it's bad to have nice things. You can surround yourself with all kinds of luxurious equipment or offices and still be successful. The main thing is to maintain focus on the goal, and see the gear as a way to provoke the desire to accomplish it, not retreat from it. It would be easy for me to use those rafts as a bed if I wasn't crystal clear on why I was here."

"Okay," Greg said. "So gear isn't the issue. I just have to be sure it helps us succeed instead of distracting us from our goal?"

"I think you got it," Sophia said. "The main thing is to have an understood goal. There has to be a "clearly defined why" that everything else serves to accomplish. All this stuff I gave you – the paddles, the raft, the vests – their only purpose is to help us get down the river safely. Gear is there to serve the goal – and the goal is what everyone needs to think about each day."

"Yeah, well for us that would be better teamwork." Greg responded.

"Teamwork is just a word. Our goal is to turn this struggling group into a GREAT team," Sophia said. "And when you leave here, you will want to agree on what your organization's compelling goal will be. Remember . . . one word is not a goal. You want to have a sentence, a memorable phrase, that defines what you and they are trying to accomplish. Keep it simple, but clear. Teamwork isn't as clear as you might think. One word can be misunderstood. So I'd like you all to think of a sentence that describes specifically what you want your people to accomplish."

She paused to emphasize her next point.

"And remember that simple takes effort, but it is much more effective than something long or complex. Don't give some academic-sounding vision statement that will go in a notebook and sits on somebody's shelf to collect dust. I want one simple phrase or sentence that explains why you guys are in business. What are you working to accomplish at CDI?"

There was silence as each of the men considered her assignment.

"You don't need to do it here, but whatever you come up with should be clear, compelling, and consistently shared. Repetition is the key to learning anything. So tell me, what is our goal today here on the river?"

"To turn us into a team," answered Cory.

"Greg, can you help him out a bit?" Sophia asked.

"To turn our struggling group into a GREAT team!" he said, with mocked enthusiasm.

"Yes, sir. That sounds better. Everybody now . . . Why are you here?"

They said it in unison, but somewhat half-heartedly. "To turn our struggling group into a GREAT team."

"Great." Said Sophia. "And it IS important to repeat it. Even if it feels a little cheesy. People need to hear it, because some in your group may not even understand it at first, and some will be on the fence and waiting to buy in completely, but the more you say it the more it becomes something they think about. And what we think about enough eventually becomes our reality. So think about what your goal is, not just for today – but for your company."

Sophia walked over to the van to talk with the driver, who had just carried a large ring of keys over to the vehicle.

Greg's people stood there in their vests, holding their paddles, waiting for her to return and give them some direction.

Tricia pulled her hair back behind her left ear and asked, "Are we ready to get started, then?"

Sophia smiled and nodded to her, then said to the group. "We'll be leaving in just a few minutes. I will be riding with you to the put-in location. We should be in the van together for about 15 or 20 minutes.

When we get in the van, I'll tell you about the second step of becoming a great team, but I want to be sure we are clear about step one."

"We've got it, Sophia," Ellis said. "Goals and Gear."

"Perfect. And why are we here today?" She held out both hands wide, with her palms up, to encourage everyone to answer.

"*To turn our struggling group into a GREAT team,*" they recited together, again with more eye-rolling than enthusiasm.

"Okay. I'll let you get away with that. Just remember . . . Goals and Gear. People need to have the right tools, but mostly they need to know why they are getting on the boat before you put it in the water and start your journey. So, whenever you have your next meeting with your people, they need to hear the sentence that you guys decide on. That'll be your homework for later. And then you will have to repeat it. A lot. Repetition is the key to learning. Ready to go?"

"Yes, ma'am," Greg said.

"But before we go, I want each of you to take a card."

Sophia reached into her backpack and pulled out a stack of laminated business cards in her left hand, offering Susan White first pick.

She looked unsure, but took one from the stack after Sophia had fanned them out.

"Don't read them yet! Your job is to get everyone to answer the question on your card, before we reach our put-in location."

Each person in the group soon had a card in hand, and all of them grinned after reading the question they had chosen.

Sophia slung the backpack onto her shoulder and motioned for everybody to get inside.

"Alright – Everybody has a question. Doesn't matter who starts, but you all have to answer each person's question before we get out . . . You'll have about twenty minutes. Okay?"

They each climbed into the van. Cory sat next to a cooler on the back bench with Tricia, and Greg sitting next to Walt in the middle row. The front row held

Susan and Andy, then Sophia closed the sliding door and hopped into the passenger side up front.

The driver started the van, and pulled out of the rafting company lot onto the two lane road.

"Oh! and there is a cooler in the back seat with your lunch," Sophia said. "Two PB & J's and a big bottled water for each of you. Alright . . . ask away!"

Greg turned and looked out the window a moment before Walt turned to Cory to ask for his two sandwiches, then said he would read his question first.

"When I'm done, we'll just go around and everybody can take turns answering, okay?"

"Just read it already," Greg laughed.

Ellis dug into the large red igloo cooler on the floorboard to distribute the sandwiches.

"Ready?" Walt smiled, as he looked down at the card to read his question to the group.

"This should be great..."

CHAPTER 6

RAPPORT
and RELATIONSHIPS

WHEN THE VAN STOPPED, they all had answered every question.

The twenty-minute ride started a bit slowly, but soon the vehicle was bursting with smiles, laughter, and unexpected facts about each of them.

As they chuckled and carried on conversations that were inspired by the question cards that Sophia had shared, she turned around to speak to the group who had suddenly become more aware of interesting information about each other.

"I need to get those cards back, but it was really fun listening to you share."

Greg looked again at the one he had been holding and then, instead of handing it to her, he motioned for each of the others to give him their cards.

"I'll collect 'em."

He eventually got all six cards in his hand, and took a moment to flip through them all to remind himself of the things they had discussed.

His card was *"What was your first job and what did you learn there?"*

Walt had asked *"What is the toughest challenge you have overcome?"*

Cory had everybody answer *"What are the three things still left on your bucket list?"*

Tricia's was *"What was your favorite childhood toy, and why?"*

Andy's card had *"What were you most afraid of when you were a kid and why?"*

And Susan's was probably the most interesting. She asked *"What is the "nerdiest" thing you do in your spare time?"*

They were obviously silly questions, but they were things that would not have come up in their normal office conversations about sales or annual reviews – and they were actually much more revealing than Greg would have thought.

He handed Sophia the six laminated cards they had used during the ride, and she put them all back into the larger stack she had drawn out of her backpack.

"It's all about connections, guys. Relationships are just an appreciation and understanding of other people's B-E-D's..."

Three of the group immediately wrinkled their brows in confusion.

Greg cocked his head to the side, wondering if he had heard her correctly.

"What did you say?" Walt asked.

"You know – their *beliefs*, their *experiences*, and their *desires*!" Sophia replied.

"If you take the time to get those three things out in the open, what you have in common with your teammates is far more influential than your differences."

She grabbed her red backpack and then opened her passenger side door. "Come on, we're almost ready to get started" she said, and she slid open the van door from the coaches.

Cory was the last to get out, and stretched a bit before he spoke.

"Hey, Sophia?"

"Yes, Mister Ellis?"

"I get that it is fun, and learning a few embarrassing or entertaining things about the people we work with, can help us feel a little bit closer to the people we work with. But how does that help us win accounts and grow profits?"

Sophia looked at each of the group members as they stood around the van.

She held her backpack over her right shoulder with her left hand.

"Great question! I guess the simple answer is that taking time to build rapport and relationships is a very powerful but the usually forgotten part of the connection process."

She waited for them to gather together before she continued her thought.

"See, there are two main ingredients to creating team unity. Think about it like an electrical plug. If one of the two prongs isn't there, you don't get any energy. You have to take time and be sure that your team has developed both parts of that electrical plug. Great teams establish a strong connection and lots of energy, because they care about two things – the goal they set, and the teammates they are working with."

Cory still didn't look convinced. "And that's what the silly question cards were for?"

"I don't think they were silly. Do you know more now about your team than you did before you got in the van? Are you more aware of what motivates them, and what they value, and how their past experiences have helped to shape them?"

He had to admit that did.

Sophia responded to his silent consent, saying "That's an important stuff!"

She put the backpack down and motioned with her arms for the group to make a circle. Then she grabbed an oar from the raft trailer and returned to the group.

"Okay – we are all standing in a circle. There are seven

of us, total. Now imagine that you have a line between you and the person you know best in the group."

She used the oar to draw three lines on the sandy ground to connect the six staff members.

"See that – all you have right now are three connections. Three lines that hold you together. But that isn't enough to survive the storms that come. Even if you have a strong connection with one or two people, that doesn't make you a great team."

She drew three more lines to connect each coach to a second person.

"Do you remember Aesop's fable about the bundle of sticks? Where the father showed his sons that a bundle of sticks cannot be broken, but when they were untied the single sticks broke easily? It's a lot like that. The more connections your team can create amongst each other…"

She drew more lines to illustrate connections between other people and soon there were lines everywhere on the ground.

"…the harder it is to tear that team apart."

She looked directly at Cory. "See, talk to any leader and they will tell you that goals and gear are important. But I am here to tell you that alone they are never enough. Rapport and relationships are vital. They are the connections to each other that allow your team to survive the conflict and adversity that you will have to overcome as part of your journey toward those goals."

She handed Ellis the oar.

"So, you guys ready to unload our raft?"

Most everyone in the group nodded and began to move to the back of the van to grab the raft.

Ellis stood still.

"Sorry, Mitch – I just don't see it," he said.

Sophia was sincerely interested. "Tell me what you're not seeing."

"Well, I know how much time our people put in at CDI. Heck, even during the off months we stay covered with paperwork and stuff to do. Are we supposed to plan time together to make sure they are all best friends, too?"

Sophia smiled.

"I understand your concern, Cory. And I agree that it can seem overwhelming. But it really doesn't have to be an off-site retreat or inconvenience people with extra work. Connections are made with simple and intentional daily conversations."

Everyone had come back to hear her finish her comments to Cory.

"Leadership and relationships occur one conversation at a time. All you and your staff need to do is to find ways to inspire people to have more conversations and interactions. Wanna know the real problem?"

She looked around the group and kept her eyes on Greg for her next comment.

The real problem is that most conversations are about authority instead of awareness. Are you giving orders or asking questions? Because, I've found that wise leaders know conversations are opportunities to connect and be curious."

She turned back to Cory.

"A young leader sees conversations as contests to be won or opportunities to showcase their own knowledge and power. As experience turns into wisdom, you realize that questions and conversations that sincerely seek to learn more about the other person are the key to building relationships."

She walked over to the raft and looked back at the group as she unhooked the first strap.

"I am just telling you what I have found to be true. Either you will have the discipline as a staff to encourage opportunities for conversations and interaction and connections, or you will have the regret of another disconnected and underachieving year."

Walt patted Cory on the back and went over to help their guide with the raft.

Susan smirked a bit of impressed laughter, and motioned to invite the other guys to help out.

Soon the raft was off the trailer and the oars were inside.

Sophia put on her life vest and suggested everyone else do the same, and then she reached back into the van for another small cooler that Greg hadn't noticed.

"Water," she said.

He nodded, and then from behind him Andy Butler asked a question. "I mentioned cliques earlier. If creating connections among all departments is important, how do we get rid of the cliques and little groups that seem to always stick together?"

"I'm glad you asked, Andy! Because I don't think cliques or silos are bad. They are just strong connections between people that have things in common."

She placed the small cooler in the raft along with her backpack and looked back at the women.

"Tricia, you and Susan are women. Because of that, we would have a natural clique. It creates rapport, because it's something we have in common. People with similar backgrounds or interests or fears or challenges – they all have a built-in rapport that allows a clique to form. The key isn't to try and destroy those cliques – the key is to create MORE of them by helping people see what they have in common so you create those lines we talked about earlier…"

She pointed at Greg.

"Greg – you love your family, right?"

"Yes, ma'am!"

"And is everything always sunshine and roses with you and your wife?"

He smiled and looked down at the ground to shake his head.

"Uh, that'd be a no. Things get a little crazy with our schedules and the kids, I guess."

"Exactly," Sophia said. "And do your managers and employees always come to work wearing a smile, because they had an amazing and encouraging morning talk with their family?"

"No ma'am – I guess not."

"So, Cory, I guess that is another reason it is important to ask those silly questions. Caring about others begins with knowing about others. Not everyone on a team has a great family at home, and if you learn that there is dysfunction in one part of someone's life, you know they need that much more support and encouragement to overcome it."

She looked back at Greg.

"But you only know that stuff, if you ask questions and build a relationship!"

"Why are you looking at me?"

"You and your staff make sales calls, don't you?"

"Sure."

"Let me ask you, when you went into a client's office as a young salesman, did you tell them all about your products and facilities and success?

"Yes."

"Do you get every sale you asked for back then?"

"Of course not – that would be impossible," Greg argued. "We're competing with so many others and there is a lot more that goes into the client decision than just..."

"I'm just asking, because if you want different results you might want to think differently. If you start to ask more about their needs and listen for what is important to them, you might get more commitments. People are more comfortable with you, and feel more important and included, if you take the time to listen to their story."

Walt Parker chimed in.

"Yeah. Their why has to be important, too, right?"

Sophia smiled.

"Right, Walt. You won't know how important every relationship is until you get into a tough spot together and have to have a difficult conversation. But the stronger the relationship, the more willing your teammate is to assume you mean well in what you are saying or doing."

Walt looked across at Greg, his longtime friend.

"Amen to that, Sophia." Walt said.

"Grab the raft, guys. I think we're ready to put in the water."

Susan replied with a polite but excited "Great!"

CHAPTER 7

EXPECATATIONS and ENCOURAGEMENT

THE RAFT WAS NEAR the edge of the water before Sophia spoke again.

"Okay, everybody, you now know the first two of our five lessons for the day. First, you need GOALS and GEAR. And second, you need to build RAPPORT and RELATIONSHIPS."

Cory Ellis was at the front of the raft holding it off the ground with his right hand.

He looked at her and then said loudly, in his best star-student voice: "And the second step is the most important of them, because it creates the connections that allow us and our teammates to say what needs to be said."

"So what's our number three lesson, Miss Mitchell," Susan White inquired.

"I'm so glad you asked." Sophia said, ". . . because, that is what will determine where you sit."

"I'm sure it does," replied Greg. He was getting used to her style of introducing lessons by now, and was willing to play along. It was entertaining, if nothing else.

"Do any of you know who Jim Collins is?"

"Yes, Mitch. We're from Nashville, not Mars!" chuckled Ellis.

"Good. Well, one of his most famous quotes is that leaders need to get 'the right people on the bus, the wrong people off the bus, and the right people in the right seats.' Do you know what he meant by that?"

"Sure. That you have to choose good people." Tricia responded.

"That's a big part of it. But the key is to define roles and establish expectations based on what those people do well. You have to get your people in the right seats."

She pointed to the raft, and continued talking.

"A high-performance team is one where everyone is contributing according to their strengths. That is why so many organizations invest in personality style assessments. They want to get good people in the right seats on their bus."

"Okay, I get that. So where do you want us to sit?", Andy asked.

"Well, part of knowing your role is realizing you are part of something bigger and more significant than yourself. The other part is doing most often what you do best – but for today, you won't need to be separated by specific skills. You will just sit two on each row, near the side. If you are left handed, you will want to sit on the left side for rowing. And you will want to sit with your foot like this."

Sophia wedged her foot underneath the side wall of the raft.

"I'll be in the back and giving you directions during our trip, and your job will be to listen and then do as I ask. I know that if my expectations aren't clear, I am setting our team up to fail. Everything that happens on the boat will be my responsibility. It is the same way for you and your company. It is unkind for leaders to be unclear..."

She paused to let the group digest that.

"Let's get her in the water and we can use the first stretch of river to go over our commands."

They carried the raft into the water, which was only a couple of feet deep at the launching spot.

They then each stepped into the raft to take their place, so three people were on each side with Sophia sitting up high on the back of the raft with her oar as their rudder.

"So, remember when I showed you how to hold your oars? The key is to understand our vocabulary and row together. Every great organization has its own vocabulary. Your company does, too. The key is to make sure everybody knows what to do in different situations, and having that cultural vocabulary helps make things much easier.

"So here is our vocabulary for today. If I say "forward paddle," everybody will row together normally. The paddler in the front left is usually the lead paddler, so Cory is who you should get in sync with. Let's try that now. Forward paddle."

The group started paddling with their oars, and soon found a common rhythm with Cory.

"Great job! Okay, 'Stop.' Now we are going to learn back paddle. All you do for that is lean forward with the oar blade pointed behind you. Then dip the blade in and pulling back with your upper hand. Ready? Back paddle."

They did well with that one also.

"Terrific. Now, if I call for a right turn, the right side back-paddles and the left side forward paddles. Let's do that one. Right turn!"

Cory, Greg, and Walt were on the left side and so they paddled forward. The other three stuck their oars in and back paddled to create the desired right turn.

"Alright! I've got a group of all-stars, don't I?" Sophia asked.

"And left turn is just the opposite, right?" Greg asked.

"You got it, Mister Sharpe – Let's try it now, just to be sure you guys are as good as you think. Okay, Left turn!"

All but Andy, who was in front on the right side, executed it perfectly. He laughed, then apologized and corrected his mistake when he realized his blunder.

"Guess I zigged, when I should have zagged," he said.

"Come on, Andy! What's wrong . . . that new hat of your on too tight for you to think?" Cory joked.

"No worries. That's what practice is for," Sophia said.

And that also brings us to my next point. Providing clear expectations about where to sit and what to do is only part of the third lesson. The other half is what to say. There is a big difference between criticism and encouragement. Criticism looks backward to blame, but encouragements and reminders look ahead and are the result of individuals claiming responsibility for team success."

Cory looked hurt. "I was just joking, Mitch!"

"I know, Cory. But it opened the door for me to talk about how to handle mistakes. Every team makes mistakes. Coaches, players, managers, and employees. Everyone. The main thing that separates great teams from their competition is how quickly and successfully they respond to those mistakes."

She paused again to let them think about that a moment.

"Did you guys get upset with an employee – or even each other – for mistakes made last year?"

Of course, the answer was yes. Each of them could recall a number of times that frustration and disappointment led to negative reactions.

Greg thought specifically of how he felt leaving their offices after his outburst at J.D., one of their salesmen. The lack of team communication and number of mistakes had led to him getting upset, and emotions had gotten the best of him.

"Okay, forward paddle. I'll talk while you work..."

They were still in a very calm and wide area of the river.

"Most of the time – unless you are working in a nuclear facility – mistakes aren't the problem. It's how people handle mistakes that create problems! So what

I want you to do, once you know your people are clear on expectations – is to clap for their mistakes."

Greg pulled his oar out of the water and turned to look at her.

"Clap? Wow, Sophie, this should be good."

"Thanks, Greg... it is. Actually CLAP is just an acronym helps to remind you to do four things, but the body movement also helps with changing your mental state. It stands for Claim responsibility, Learn from it, Affirm your ability, and Play on."

She surveyed the water and decided that she had enough time to talk it through.

"First, claim responsibility. You can't fix it if you don't own it. Instead of blaming, change the question. Ask yourself how your leadership led to that outcome. Then, learn from it. Really think about how to keep it from happening again. If you and your team stop making the same mistakes over and over, it's amazing what you will accomplish."

She let them row a couple times before continuing.

"Third, affirm your ability. Don't let one mistake derail your confidence or competitive edge. Tell yourself that's not how you do things and remember past positives. And last, play on. Focus on the next play. It's not only football or basketball that are next play sports. Life is about moving on and using mistakes as fuel for improvement. Stop!"

They all took their oars out of the water.

"Great work, everyone. We can coast a minute, and then I'll get you ready for our first test."

"Clap, huh?" asked Walt.

"Yes, sir. But the secret is to learn to clap when things aren't going well. If we are going with a boat metaphor, a captain's job is to lead through storms, not through sunny days. Anybody can paddle with confidence when it's 75 degrees and sunny. When you clap for mistakes, it's about making yourself accountable and keeping things positive and encouraging."

Tricia spoke up excitedly, "so the third part of your recipe is to share EXPECTATIONS AND ENCOURAGEMENT?"

"Exactly," Sophia said proudly.

Cory thoughtfully shook his head. "Well, I'm not sure I agree."

"Okay . . . why not?"

"Well, I am in charge of scheduling and coordinating installations and crews. We set expectations and we teach our people how to do things the right way. And yes, I get the importance of goals and relationships . . . but clapping isn't going to get my guys to lift and move furniture as hard as they need to."

"I understand, Cory. Every team has members who are not as self-motivated as others. Go into any office building in America and you'll see the same thing there. That's why leaders delegate and inspect."

"I'm listening..."

All six of them listened intently, although only a couple of them would turn their heads back to show their full attention was on Sophie's words.

"Whether its athletes or teachers or salesmen, I would encourage you to develop your hardest workers into peer leaders. If you have addressed a problem with someone, and it hasn't improved, find somebody else who has shown he can lead himself and ask that person to be responsible for the teammate. The way to develop people is to delegate responsibility . . .

"Imagine there are two kids at a table. Kid one cleans his plate of all vegetables just like you asked, and the other chooses not to. When it comes time for dessert, only kid one gets ice cream. But the next night, you want the other kid to clean his plate of vegetables, too. So, you change things a bit and now only give kid one ice cream, if kid two cleans his plate. You delegate and involve other people to get the job done. When you are on a team, you are responsible for more than just yourself. You're 200 percent responsible. We have to be responsible for our raft-mates as well, because everybody sinks or swims together."

"And what if kid two still refuses to eat the vegetables?" Greg asked.

"Then somebody else needs to be given that seat at the table. That goes back to the idea of getting the right people on your bus. Sometimes, you need to let people off the bus to make room and get the right people on it."

"I like this lady," Ellis smiled. "This could be more fun than I thought!"

Sophia looked ahead of them to survey the river.

"Well, don't pin a medal on me yet. I'm not some million dollar consultant. I'm just a basketball manager turned river guide who has learned a few things about what makes great teams work."

"So you're not raking in big money here to help pay for college?" Andy asked.

"Ha. Nope, I'm not a river guide for the money. I think the best part of my job as guide is that I get to help create more guides. Maybe not here on the river, but there's lots of places that need more effective guides. Anyway, most of us have to get other part time jobs. Hey – you know how to get a river guide off your front porch?"

The coaches looked at each other and then shook their heads.

"You pay for the pizza!" Sophia laughed at her joke. "Ha, I love that one!"

They all chuckled.

"Now, we do have a minute or two before we get to Patton's Run. The Nantahala starts with a class three rapid to get attention, then provides opportunities for growth and learning and finishes with two class three rapids to test you at the end. And one last thing…"

Sophia pointed at the water underneath them.

"There are two kinds of rafters; those who have fallen out and those who someday will. The water will be a crisp 42 degrees, but if you do fall out of the raft, don't panic! If you are in moving water, just flip over and float on your back with your feet facing downstream and toes up to the sky. If you are close enough for us to pull you back in, only one person will do it. If you are the closest to the swimmer then you are the rescuer."

The group looked around at each other and then at the water and trees and the mountains that surrounded the river they were on.

"To pull someone back in, you use your body weight and both arms. Put both knees on the side of the raft facing the swimmer, then grab the life jacket at the shoulders and pull up and while you fall back into the boat with the other person."

She illustrated by reaching over the side of the raft to grab an imaginary persons vest at the shoulders, and then leaning back.

"Just like we talked about – when a mistake is made, your job is to pick your teammates back up! Alright, here we go – forward paddle, guys."

They started paddling together. Walt quietly noticed how in sync they had become.

Sophia kept talking.

"Just remember, Goals and Gear, Rapport and Relationships, then Expectations and Encouragements. Expectations are nothing more than work agreements – like the stuff I talked to you guys about when we first started paddling. I made sure to be clear about our vocabulary, about who was supposed to do what, and when. And then I set expectations for what to do when things go wrong – because they always do. That's why we have teammates – to pick us up and encourage us up and encourage us through challenges."

She let them enjoy the scenery for a moment before sharing a bit of trivia.

"So, the history of the area is actually pretty interesting. The word 'Nantahala' comes from the Cherokee Indians and means 'Land of the Noonday Sun.'"

She pointed to the high cliffs above them.

"The river runs through a steep gorge where the sun only reaches some parts of the ground if it is directly overhead during the middle of the day. Okay – see that rock up there – we want to stay to the right of it. So, right turn..."

Cory and the two people behind him paddled forward, while Andy and his side backward paddled in unison.

The turn went smoothly, and Sophia congratulated them.

"Nice paddling, everybody – That was great!"

CHAPTER 8

ROUGH WATERS

THE RIVER MADE A slight right turn and curved around the wall of trees that rose up above them.

Their guide kept her eyes on the challenge ahead.

"Okay, now forward paddle again. Up here on the left is the rock we want to stay away from. We're coming up on Patton's Run!"

Greg could see the two large rocks jutting out of on the left side of the river, and the water rolling and frothing and turning white as it hit the smaller rocks and the drop-off on the right.

The current seemed to carry the raft toward the rocks that Sophie had mentioned, and Greg felt himself energized and enjoying the outdoors and the exhilaration of the moment.

"Right turn, people!" she called out.

Ellis, Sharpe, and Parker all dug their oars into the water and paddled hard, but the three paddlers on the right side of the raft hesitated a few seconds.

By the time they had begun to try and help, instead of a smooth right turn the raft began to spin around wildly.

The rocks were approaching more quickly than Greg had thought.

He soon realized that the current and their direction would send them directly into a collision with the obstacle their guide had warned them about.

"Okay, then . . . hold on!" Sophie smirked.

The raft had twisted so that by the time it hit the flatter of the two rocks that was near the middle of the river, the front of the raft was no longer in front. When they hit, it was the back corner of the raft, near Tricia.

They bounced off the rock and the raft spun again, turning them around and sending the high splash of white water directly at Cory as they were pushed to the right side of the river where they had intended to go in the first place.

Sophie worked the back of the raft with her oar, trying to steady it.

The group of coworkers yelled and laughed as most of them got wet from the spray, and in only a few moments that part of the river was behind them again and they were in calmer water.

Sophia spoke as they shook the water from themselves.

"Patton's Run is the first rapid on the River. That rock formation on the left side of the river is known as 'Jaws.' If we had been a few feet further to the left when we hit, we could've gotten stuck there. Water's cold, huh?"

"Wow – it sure is!" Susan replied, smiling.

"If you were a basketball team, I would tell you that was like a tough preseason scrimmage game. It's a first test, and comes early so you can see what needs to be fixed. That is one of the things I like about the Nantahala – you start off with a fun class three like Patton's Run, then you get to have a little fun and enjoy yourself a while until you finish up with another more challenging class three rapid at Nantahala Falls."

"That wasn't too bad," Greg shared.

"Naw – that was fun," Andy echoed.

"Well, we did hit the rock…" Walt answered.

Greg looked over his shoulder with a scowl at the man who had been critical of him in the meeting room earlier, and before that with the President of the company.

"Walt, we're here to have fun. You don't have to find fault everywhere." Greg exhaled through his nose and then finished his thought. "It was just a little bump. The current pushed us over there, but we made it just fine."

Walt looked across at Tricia, then back to Sophia, for support.

"The current is just an easy excuse, Greg. The current is like the weather or the economy. It's just something we have to deal with as a team – but it can't be an excuse for us not doing our jobs well."

"Walt, buddy, you're making this too big a deal." Greg's volume rose to stay above the churning sound of the water around them.

"Well, we're not just here to have fun," Walt said.

"Really?" Greg responded. His voice was sharper now than it had been.

"Little things turn into big things," Walt countered. "You can't make excuses and choose what you want to ignore. We're here, because we need to become a better team, remember?'

Greg thought back to his conversation with Patterson, but he still bristled at the idea that Walt was being so critical of him.

"Okay, Sophia. You tell me…" Greg said. "Was that twist of ours something to get upset about?"

Sophia knew this was an important part of their trip, and a very influential conversation.

"I don't think that complaining ever solves much of anything…"

Greg started to nod his head in perceived victory.

"BUT…"

All six held their oars above the water and waited for her comments.

"I do believe that this trip becomes a microcosm of your company interactions. It is a tiny little example, but how you do anything is how you do most everything. And if you are in the habit of blaming the current, you won't be interested in finding and fixing that part of yourself that caused or contributed to the experience."

Greg's chin and shoulders fell and he stared into the bottom of the raft.

"Perfect," he mumbled.

Then he spoke up, louder. "So we can't have a good time? I mean, it's like three feet of water, right guys?"

Before nodding in agreement, the others looked to Sophia again.

"There was a teenager that fell out, got her foot caught, and drowned in that three feet of water a few years ago. There are hundreds of rocks that are slightly submerged, so you really don't get to see most of the danger, until you are past it. Like I said, how people handle this journey is a lot like how they handle their projects or their seasons."

"Everything matters," Susan said – to nobody in particular.

"What do you mean, Susan?" asked Greg.

"I mean, Walt is right. You can't blame the current. We didn't use our oars."

Before Greg could reply, Sophia was pulling a Ziploc bag out of her backpack – and passed it around. It was filled with an assortment of candy bars and granola bars.

"Enjoy a snack. You guys are doing really well so far." Sophia said, then she placed the bag back inside her large red backpack and pointed down-river, ahead of them.

"This next part is called Tumble Dry. There is a little island in the middle of the river. Below that is a series of small rocks and rapids that will bounce us around enough so you can 'tumble dry' after getting splashed by Patton's Run. This is a place where we can play a bit. I'll usually get the group to spin around and do a 360 here with one side rowing forward, and the other side rowing backward."

"So do you guys think I make excuses?" Greg changed the subject back.

Walt didn't want to be the one to speak up again.

Thankfully, there were two others that spoke up.

"Greg, there will always be a current of some kind," Andy said. "We just have to learn to get our people to row together."

Cory joined him. "It's like she said about blame, Greg. That policy you want to put in might be a good one – but it isn't the only thing we need to change. Maybe we should be looking at ourselves more."

Greg was stunned. Could his staff see something he didn't?

"Alright, guys – the water isn't super deep here" said Sophia, "so we have to be careful not to get stuck. If you feel the raft get caught, we're going to popcorn."

"That sounds fun," Tricia smiled. She tucked a strand of hair behind her left ear.

"It's easy, too... If we get stuck in a shallow spot you just bounce up and down like kernels of corn that are popping. That should free the raft and help us get moving again."

About that time, the raft began to slow down through a shallow part.

"Let's do it! Popcorn time!" Walt said, trying to lighten the mood.

The group grudgingly started to bounce, standing and sitting on the inflated raft, and all but Greg were soon smiling again.

Greg was moving to free the raft, but remained thoughtful.

"I think we do a good job, Greg," Walt said. "But I think we can be better."

Greg sat down, and was abruptly bounced six inches off the raft when it hit a rock.

He grabbed for Walt to keep himself in the boat, and nearly fell out.

It made him smile.

"Maybe this is the shake-up I needed, huh?" He smiled at his longtime friend.

Greg then looked at Cory and the others. "Well, from now on I promise not to blame the current. Let's make today about…"

He and his staff were bounced up off their seats again.

He smiled warmly at Sophia, then finished his thought.

"Let's make today about fixing us."

He turned to the back of the raft.

"Okay, Sophie. So far you've talked about GOALS and GEAR, then about RAPPORT and RELATIONSHIPS, and the third lesson was EXPECTATIONS and EN-COURAGEMENTS. What else is there?" Greg asked.

"Do any of you really like to cook?" she asked.

Walt chuckled.

"Does the microwave count?" asked Andy.

Cory wiped a wet hand on his purple t-shirt sleeve. "I do some grilling now and then."

Only Tricia seemed proud of her talents. "Yes ma'am. I know my way around a kitchen. That's one thing my momma taught me well."

Sophia made a wide circle with her right index finger above her head to indicate the river and their natural surroundings.

"What we're doing out here…" She put her hand back on the oar and continued to steer. "…is nothing more than giving you a great recipe.

If you want a great meal, you have to add all the right ingredients. You can't make my mom's chocolate chip cookies without all five parts. You have to have the butter, flour, sugar, egg, and chocolate chips. Leave any of them out, and you don't get the same result."

She looked ahead of them as she talked.

"Forward paddle, guys."

They did.

"Great teams are the same way. The word GREAT is another acronym. Great teamwork is an easy recipe, but if you leave out any of the ingredients, or add them in the wrong order, you won't get the results you want. We've got a few minutes before we get to the next challenge. I guess you guys are ready for ingredient number four…"

"This next part starts with an A, doesn't it?" asked Greg.

Sophia smiled and nodded.

Greg responded with a smile. "Great."

CHAPTER 9

ACCOUNTABILITY
and ADJUSTMENTS

"SEE THAT?"

Sophia pointed at the water, where Andy's paddle had been. "That's the next ingredient in our recipe for great teams."

"Ripples?" asked Walt.

"Or hitting people with paddles?" joked Cory.

"Yes, Walt . . . I meant the ripples!" Sophia quickly explained. "Ripples are evidence of impact. So, the next thing on our list of things that all great teams have in common is a culture of accountability and willingness to make adjustments."

"ACCOUNTABILITY AND ADJUSTMENTS, huh? Okay – I'll ask. How are ripples like accountability?" Greg smiled at Walt as he asked the question.

"Accountability," Sophia answered, "is about understanding the impact of your efforts. It isn't about punishment – it's empathy that inspires people to become more accountable."

Sophia looked ahead down the river a ways before deciding to continue her comments.

"Most people think that accountability is providing consequences for meeting or not meeting expectations. But real accountability isn't ever the result of punishment or reward. Yes, you need to have consequences . . . but true accountability is created with emotional connections and an understanding of how your actions impact others . . ."

Greg had begun to enjoy Sophia's lessons, and even felt himself agreeing with her explanations up to this point, so he hesitated to disagree with her.

But Cory was far less patient with his rebuttal.

"Wait, Sophie…" Cory shook his head in disbelief. "Are you saying that we shouldn't have consequences to inspire certain behaviors?

Sophie nodded. "That is exactly what I am saying…"

"That's nuts," he said, and looked away from her, toward Greg.

"Really? Well, you're a pretty ambitious guy. Early thirties, heading up your own department. So, why do you do what you do?"

He looked back at her and the sun made him squint.

"What do you mean?"

She politely rephrased her question. "I mean, what motivates you to work hard? Is it fear of consequences, or something else?"

"Well, I don't want to lose my job and my house. So yeah – I'm motivated by consequences."

"I think it might be more than that, Cory. In my experience, people are either unwilling, complaint or committed. The unwilling get rid of themselves. Most people are compliant. They do just enough to get by or to keep clear of those consequences you're referring to. But committed people aren't concerned with consequences. They are focused on ripples."

She pointed down at the water, where Andy's paddle was moving.

"They think about the impact their actions have on the others," she concluded.

Cory paused and thought a moment before responding.

Tricia chuckled and shared a smile with Susan.

"Alright. Well . . . I guess..." Cory stammered a bit.

Sophia interrupted him. "You guys aren't wrong to have consequences. I was just pulling your chain..."

Now Cory looked totally confused.

"I know we live in the real world and not everyone is as driven as you may be. Even when I was the team manager, Coach Patterson thought it was important to measure and publish the numbers he felt was important. But he also knew that people would game the system and manipulate stats if they weren't motivated to do more than just comply."

Greg's ears perked up as he heard her mention numbers. That is what so many of his people were bothered by – his insistence on metrics and measuring performance.

"So measuring performance isn't bad, Sophia?"

"Not at all, Greg. But Patterson used to joke about stats, also. He said that statistics were a lot like bikinis.

They never tell the whole story!"

Walt laughed out loud at that.

"Forward paddle, guys," Sophia ordered.

They rowed in unison without noticing their own improved technique.

"Yeah, but he agreed that you have to measure and hold people accountable for their numbers, right?" Greg pleaded.

Sophia thought a bit.

"I don't think you can hold people accountable, Greg," she said. "That is my point with Cory. I think we choose to be accountable individually based upon our understanding of how our actions affect other people. It is empathy that drives accountability – and that requires relationships."

Andy pulled his paddle out of the water and jumped into the conversation.

"Okay, Sophia . . . if accountability is internal, then all we can do, according to you, is provide consequences. But that isn't accountability. So how do we improve accountability?"

"Well, I think you do need consequences – everything we do has consequences. But as a leader, you inspire accountability by helping people see the ripples. That is why the recipe I'm sharing is given in a specific order. Rules without relationships lead to rebellion. People only follow rules when they understand the impact that breaking them might have on people they care about."

Andy nodded and remained quiet.

Then, Susan spoke up.

"So, as leaders, how do we improve accountability, Ms. Mitchell?"

Sophia turned her body a bit to address Susan.

"You improve it like anything else. One conversation and one action at a time. But people have to build relationships and see the connections between what they do and what other people do and the more awareness you can build about each other and the roles you play and why you depend on each other, the more you will see people considering those things and acting more responsibly – because nobody wants to let down somebody they care about."

"I'm having a conversation with an employee, then," Greg broke in.

They all looked over at him.

The sun was warm and a lone bird chirped from a tree somewhere on their left.

"And as part of that conversation, I go through their quarterly numbers and they are lower than they should be. What are you saying I need to do to make them more accountable?"

"That's a great question, Greg," she replied. "Let me ask you a question back. If it was you in the other chair, and your boss was talking about your numbers, and you felt like he was blaming you for something . . . how would you feel?"

"How would I feel? I'd feel like I needed to do better. I'd take responsibility."

"Or you'd make excuses," Cory said. "That's what some people do when they get defensive"

Greg waited to hear Sophia's response.

"Cory is right. I think if you focus on numbers, you lose people. But if you focus on people, you get your numbers! It isn't about blame, though. That's the key. Left turn, everybody"

They had begun to drift a bit toward the shore and some low hanging branches, but soon were back in the middle of the river floating safely.

"Okay – forward paddle... And rest a bit." She continued, "What I learned from Patterson is that our focus should always be on finding solutions and letting people know you are there to help, not affixing blame and making them feel like they are being attacked."

"So if something is wrong, I can't tell them? I think if there is an elephant in the room, we need to acknowledge it!" Greg said.

"I agree. But your intent is the key. Think of your ripples. How you paddle determines the kind of ripples you create. If your intent is to help people succeed, that will look and feel a lot different than looking for things to criticize and blame. People don't mind talking truths and naming elephants as long as they feel like we are there to help them with taming them. Our accountability conversations should focus on developing people, not punishing them."

"So what would a productive accountability conversation look like to you?" Greg asked,

"Well, Coach Patterson used to say that feedback was the breakfast of champions. The only way we improve our performance is to get quality feedback, so we can see the gap that exists between where we are and where we might be…"

The six directors were all listening intently.

Sophia continued to speak to Greg, keeping her eyes alternately on him and on the river.

"Good accountability conversations begin long before the conversation. They start with everyone agreeing on a shared goal, and they get much easier when you have built enough of a relationship that the person you are talking to feels safe instead of threatened. But the most important part of an accountability conversation is identifying the elephant, whatever the behavior or issue is, and then describing how it affected the people inside or outside of your organization. Once you do that, you assume the best and ask what they think led to the behavior and how you can support them in closing the gap from where they are to where they could be."

"So naming the elephant isn't the problem …" Greg said, looking for her agreement. "You're saying I just need to make people feel like I'm there to help them instead of judge them."

"I think you got it," she said. "And we're coming up to our next challenge now…"

"What is this one called?" asked Andy.

"This is called 'whirlpool rapid,' because the river makes a right hand turn and creates a giant swirl of water from the center of the river over to the left bank." She pointed at the curve in the river ahead. "The current will try to push us to the right, but if we paddle hard we can whip our raft over into the eddy on the left and have some fun spinning around."

"Sounds like fun!" Walt announced.

"Okay, left turn, people!" Sophia ordered, with a smile.

Their paddles dug into the water, and Greg noticed the ripples.

Soon the raft had been propelled into the whirlpool, and the group laughed and held on as the water twisted them around clockwise.

It was fun. Nobody spoke – they just enjoyed the moment together.

And then Sophia's voice called out again. "Alright, here we go . . . Paddle forward!"

They did, and soon they had left the whirlpool and were traveling again down the middle of the slow moving current.

"That wasn't tough at all – it was fun," Tricia announced.

"Yeah – good stuff. Thanks, Sophia." Cory said.

"You guys were terrific back there. That only becomes a challenge, if people aren't alert and working together. It's easy to get stuck longer than you mean to if somebody is stubborn or doing their own thing . . ."

"Why wouldn't paddlers listen to you?" asked Walt.

"Good question. But whether it's paddlers on the water or players on a court or employees in an office, not everybody is willing to listen and make adjustments when they need to. Patterson said that it was usually an ego that got in the way."

"Ego?" asked Greg.

"Yeah. You know what ego does, right?" Sophia asked? They waited for her punchline.

"It eliminates growth opportunities."

"So ego is a bad thing?" asked Cory.

"It definitely can be. Good ego is believing that you have skills to contribute. Bad ego is arrogance – it means you aren't willing to learn and grow."

Sophia went back to her point. "Let's say you have one of those accountability conversations, and you point out an elephant that needs to be tamed. People who are made aware of an issue have a choice – they can change and improve, or they can dig in and get defensive."

Walt looked at Greg, who nodded back at his friend in understanding.

"Most of the time," Sophia continued, "defensiveness is the result of fear – that's why you have to make your conversations safe and ensure your teammates know you are there to help them get better. If they aren't willing to adjust, that's when you get other people to help them eat their vegetables."

"Whoa – too many metaphors!" Andy yelled.

"You know, the vegetables and ice cream example she gave us back when we were talking about expectations and encouragements," Greg reminded him.

"Sounds like consequences to me," Cory said, flashing a clever smile at Sophia.

"You're right – just remember that consequences don't drive commitment. Consequences rarely do more than teach people to be compliant."

Andy pulled his paddle out of the water.

"So tell us more about adjustments. How do you get people to see they need to change?"

"Well, first, I would say that you can't change others. But if you change yourself and how you approach and interact with others, that has a huge impact. Our tone, our words, our actions can help to create a culture of personal accountability if you frame things the right way."

"Okay...we're listening. How do you suggest people do that?" Greg asked.

"When we won or lost a game," Sophia answered, "Patterson had players write down the 2–3 reasons WHY they thought it happened on an index card. Then he had them write down what needed to happen to fix it on the back. Sometimes the ones that needed to adjust weren't aware of how they were hurting the team, and needed to be convinced – that's when he would meet with them individually and show them the stats or the video they needed to see. But the key was always to help them see how their actions impacted the team."

Sophia paused, to survey the river before continuing. Walt rubbed his goatee and pulled his Aussie hat further down on his forehead.

"Patterson also made sure that the accountability conversations he had did more than just identifying an elephant, though. He always finished by focusing the player on how to tame it and offered his assistance. One of our guards was shooting too many threes and had a poor field goal percentage, so coach had him list ways to make it better. Because he wanted to be a shooter, the kid got in the gym and took an extra 300 shots every morning until he made 50% consistently to earn a green light. Patterson had his players commit to taking specific action, because he knew that changed behaviors would lead to changed results..."

"And if those accountability conversations didn't lead to them making adjustments and changing behaviors?" Greg asked.

"Then there were consequences. But, if you are clear about expectations, and consistent with your intention to cultivate people and not just criticize them, the entire team will know that you've done what you could and tried to help tame the elephant. If people are stubborn, and full of bad ego, you deal with it."

"Deal with it how?" asked Walt.

"Well, if someone is unhappy, unproductive, and unwilling to change, Patterson would say that the best thing a leader can do is to set them free to find a better fit elsewhere. If there's a squeaky wheel somewhere, you either repair it or you replace it. But you never ignore it."

"I like this girl," Walt said.

"So do I," said Greg. He gave her a thumbs up.

"Well, Ms. Mitchell, I suppose we are ready for your last lesson, then," said Susan.

Sophia grinned and said, "Great!"

CHAPTER 10

TOASTS and TRANSFER

"WE'RE COMING UP ON the end of our ride to-gether. Only have a couple more challenges left before we reach our put-out spot. First comes 'the bump,' and then we finish with Nantahala Falls," Sophia announced.

"So, what is the last part of your acronym?" Greg asked.

"Yeah – better hurry up and tell us if we're close to the end of our trip!" said Cory.

"Okay, guys . . . I'll tell you. Of course, you know they start with the letter T. But first, tell me this. Did any of you ever have a Game Boy?"

"I heard of 'em, but never..." Walt replied.

"Yeah, I had one," interjected Andy.

"Me too," said Cory. "Loved playing Tetris, man . . . and Zelda! Good times!"

"Right. It was a handheld video game." Sophia ex-plained. "Something we played with before everybody had a cell phone, remember?"

"First time I ever played Madden Football was on a Game Boy!" Andy shared.

"Okay, we know what you're talking about. What about 'em, Sophia?" asked Greg.

"Well, I loved mine. It was purple . . . and I carried it everywhere," Sophia stared off into the sky, as if remembering her youth and the joy of the white plastic electronic games she played. "But it didn't always work. Sometimes it just quit."

Tricia frowned. "So what was wrong with it?"

"Oh, nothing was wrong with it," Sophia shared. "Sometimes it just needed new batteries!"

She waited a moment to see if her example had resonated with them.

It apparently hadn't, because only blank looks stared back at her expectant face.

"You see, for me then, and for you now, double-A batteries are the best energizer in the world!"

"Okay, you lost me Sophia," Andy complained.

"It's about the last part of the acronym for being a GREAT team. Double-A batteries are just a way to remember part of the recipe I've been describing today. You have to applaud and appreciate the people you work with!"

She paused again to see if they had connected the dots.

"Uugh. Fine . . . The last part of the recipe is TOASTS and TRANSFER. You have to toast your teammates. Applause and appreciation can fuel people for months . . . you know . . . like a game boy only runs if it has AA batteries?"

They all began nodding their heads. It made sense now.

"Guess I need to work on that last metaphor to make it clearer what I'm talking about," Sophia admitted.

"Guess so. But I like it. Toast your teammates and make sure they feel appreciated, right?" confirmed Walt.

"Yes, sir. Honest praise or a specific grateful observation can have an incredible impact on your teammates. Mark Twain once said he could live two months on a good compliment. But there are a bunch of leaders," Sophia explained, "who don't realize how important and powerful praise can be. I bet Patterson would tell you that used to be one of his biggest problems."

"Really?" remarked Greg, interested in hearing more.

"Oh, sure. Forward paddle, guys. We're coming up on the bump – it's not too far ahead. You're gonna see an orange and yellow sign that says "Bump" to warn people. Let's make sure we stay on the right side of the river where there is a small set of waves. It'll give us a bouncy ride, but won't be as dangerous as the large ledge on the left side that bumps a lot of people out of their raft!"

"Right turn?" asked Greg.

"Yep . . . right turn . . . good. Okay, enjoy the ride over these waves!"

They bounced along the right side and soon were past the area.

"So, yeah. Patterson was a really good coach – but he wasn't always the most generous with praise. For all the stuff I learned from him, that's the one thing I think he might have learned from me. I knew the team needed to hear compliments before we got to the end of season banquet – but Patterson wasn't always tuned in to that."

Sophia shook her hand to emphasize the next point...

"Of course, today, he probably overdoes it. Once he saw how it affected the guys, he swore by it. The last year I was with him, he swore that it was the reason we did so well as a team. He even kept a post-it note on his bulletin board that said 'what gets rewarded gets repeated.'"

"Yeah, we put in a reward program at CDI." Greg commented.

"That's good," Sophia said. "Because recognition and retention of good employees is supposedly the main challenge for employers over the next few years. But, there is a big difference between a plan and a priority. Just because you think you are doing it well doesn't mean your people have the same perception. I know that for Coach Patterson, that was the issue. He thought the banquet was enough – and my candy bars changed his mind."

"You gave out candy bars when you were a manager?" asked Andy, adjusting his orange cap.

"Sure did. I could tell the guys needed little pick-me-ups along the way even if Patterson didn't . . . so I started bringing in candy bars sometimes to celebrate stuff. It seems silly, but it made a big difference in their attitude."

"Don't berate . . . Celebrate!" Tricia observed.

"Yeah! That's perfect, Tricia... and research keeps showing that positive reinforcement drives performance and moves people from compliance to commitment. But it can't just be a plan. The end of season banquet was a plan. You have to make recognition a priority and find ways to toast your teammates for little things along the way. Make sure they feel appreciated and applauded for their efforts and accomplishments. Because, if they don't feel valued, they are surely going to go somewhere else sometime soon."

"I can agree with that," said Tricia. "When they don't feel appreciated, people start thinking of leaving."

Greg knew that Tricia was thinking of more than just at the office. "Then maybe we should look at our reward program and see how we can improve it."

"It's not just about a program, though," Sophia warned him. "It's a way of seeing things. It's looking to catch people doing things right, and not waiting for the end of the month or end of the quarter to mention or reward it. It's about knowing what your teammates like and not doing the same thing for different people. That's why, I didn't insist on giving everybody a Baby Ruth. They might be MY favorite, but some people are allergic. And some don't even like chocolate!"

"That's just crazy talk," joked Tricia.

"I know, right?" Sophia laughed.

"Okay . . . I get it," Greg said. "Toasts are important – and not just at the end of a project. So tell us about transfer. What's that about?"

"What do you think your next job will be, Greg?"

"Huh? I...uh . . . haven't thought about it," Greg responded. "We're trying to make sure I do a good enough job after today to keep the one I have at CDI right now!"

"That may be true . . . but usually people have an idea of what they want to do or where they'd like to move next, whether they really make the move or not. But today, most every job is a stepping stone to something else. I don't think many people would argue with me for saying that destination positions are almost non-existent these days..."

She waited for any rebuttal from the group, but none came. They were waiting for her to explain the transfer part of this recipe she was almost done sharing.

"I think the last thing you need to do as a leader is to help your people grow and get better and add skills, and carry away those leadership lessons into their next position. That's the transfer I'm talking about. When people have to leave, what memory of you will they leave with? What values and beliefs and skills will you pour into them, so they are better for having had you in their life?"

"It's not just about numbers..." Greg said.

"I don't think so, Mister Sharpe," Sophia said, soberly.

"That's my challenge, then," he replied.

Sophia looked ahead of them and pointed to the left side of the river.

"That's our last challenge today! Nantahala Falls is the final rapid we'll encounter. It's a pretty swift moving class three, and it's the most exciting and popular rapid on the river. We'll need to approach it on the left side where there is some swiftly moving water…"

She nodded to them all to confirm they understood what to do.

"Okay, then. Left turn, team!"

The men and women paddled as instructed.

"This rapid is a lot of fun," Sophia promised. "And there'll be a photographer on the photo deck above us to capture your faces so you can remember the day…"

Their paddling had carried them to the left side, and the quick current jostled them along faster than they had anticipated toward a large splash as the raft moved beyond Nantahala Falls.

"Awesome!" Cory yelled.

"Woooo!" Tricia screamed.

Walt and the others chuckled and held up their paddles, victorious.

Sophia coached them as they rowed over to the bank where they saw others step onto the shore and drag their raft out of the water.

They had made it.

Susan and Tricia walked together up the bank. Cory, Walt, and Sophia stood together and watched Greg help Andy pull the raft out of the river.

Greg smiled as they passed Sophia, and said, "That was great!"

CHAPTER 11

KNOWING AND DOING

"I'M STARVING!" CORY ANNOUNCED to everyone.

They had made their way back up the slight hill at the take-out spot and loaded the raft onto the trailer and were ready to get back to the rafting company location. According to Sophia, it was only a couple of minutes away.

"I know you guys are ready to dry off," Sophia mentioned, "and get something to eat. We should have the bar-b-que lunches that Greg ordered waiting for you in the picnic area when we arrive back at the outpost."

"Alright, Greg!" Andy said.

Everyone climbed into the van and Sophia checked the raft tie-downs, secured the vests and paddles, and spoke a minute with the driver before joining them. Her backpack was slung over her right shoulder as she turned to talk to them.

"We should also have a CD with pictures of your group at Nantahala Falls for each of you. That is the other part of the package he paid for . . . but it isn't the last part of what I wanted to share with you."

The driver pulled forward on the gravel road, and the van bounced a bit on the uneven surface.

"What else do you have for us, Miss Mitchell?" inquired Susan.

Greg looked curiously in her direction, awaiting her reply.

"It's the last thing I have in my backpack," Sophia explained, "that I want to share with you guys. We should be back in just a minute or two and I'll say more there while you guys are eating."

She was right.

The van pulled off of highway 74 into the driveway of the rafting company less than a minute later. The group scrambled out of the vehicle toward the Chevy Tahoe they had driven up in and grabbed bags of dry clothes to change into, for their late lunch and drive back home.

Barely ten minutes later, the entire group was sitting together at a picnic table, revived by freshly washed faces and new sets of clothes, although Andy still wore the orange cap that he had purchased in the store that morning.

Sophia let them eat by themselves for a few minutes, then emerged from the store with her backpack still on her shoulder and a couple of items in her left hand. When she arrived, they could see that she was holding a small cardboard package, about the size of a book, and a manila envelope.

She placed the cardboard package on the picnic table next to Susan, dropped her backpack to the ground, and then turned to face the group, still holding the letter-sized envelope.

"Susan has your picture CD's from the trip today. I figure she will get them back safely and be sure everyone gets a copy!"

Susan smiled and nodded her willingness to do that.

"So, what are you guys going to remember from today?" Sophia asked the group.

"I'll take this one," Walt answered. "We learned the recipe for building a GREAT team... Ready everybody?"

Walt raised his index finger as a cue to the rest of them.

"GOALS AND GEAR," they said, in unison.

Walt showed two fingers, and the group responded...

"RAPPORT AND RELATIONSHIPS," they recited.

Then he held up three fingers...

"EXPECTATIONS AND ENCOURAGEMENTS," they continued.

And then four...

"ACCOUNTABILITY AND ADJUSTMENTS!" They had grown progressively louder.

And finally, all of Walt's fingers were outstretched...

The group yelled, "TOASTS AND TRANSFER!"

Sophia smiled wide, surprised with their enthusiasm.

"That was great, everybody. I guess you do know the acronym and the recipe for building a great team. But knowing that isn't why you came here today. Do you remember what we talked about this morning?"

Greg nodded his head, remembering the shed they had spent time in, the questions they had asked on the van ride, and the other interesting and unexpected lessons that Sophia had shared over the last few hours on the water.

"Yes, ma'am," Andy replied.

"Alright, Andy. Why did you come here?"

"We made this trip to turn this struggling group into a GREAT team," he answered.

"And so are you a great team now?"

Andy looked to Greg.

Greg started to nod his head. He wanted to believe that the day had been a success.

But he knew that, if he was being honest with himself, the answer was no.

"Not yet..." he admitted, almost ashamedly.

The others seemed a bit disheartened by his reply.

"I'm so glad you said that!" Sophia beamed.

She had surprised them all again.

"What do you mean? You're glad he said no?" Cory asked.

"Thrilled!" Sophia said. "If he had said yes, it wouldn't have been true. Because you're not a team yet. And that is my last lesson for all of you before you have to head back.

"Then why did we go on the trip? What were we doing out there together?" Cory asked, incredulous.

"What I mean is that it's great you all know the recipe, but it is a whole lot more important that you chose to follow it. There is a huge difference between knowing and doing. If all you did was learn, then I wasted your time. I want you to do something different, because of what you learned. Applying lessons is the most important part of learning them."

"Well . . . okay. That makes sense," Cory shrugged.

Walt chuckled at his backpedalling.

"My job is to be sure that you don't treat today like buying life insurance – where you pay for it, but never want to use it. Don't just keep this information inside you." The manila envelope shook in her hand as Sophia spoke. "I want you to apply the information and take action. If nothing changes, then nothing changes. And if you guys remember our conversations about the company illnesses and who drugged the water and what the antidote should be, the worst thing that could happen in your organization is nothing!"

"So, we'll work through each of the five parts of the recipe together. Do you have ideas or anything written down," Tricia asked, "that will help us do that when we are back at the office?"

"I'm glad you asked, Tricia. Turns out I do!"

Sophia held out the manila envelope and offered it to Greg.

"What's this?" Greg asked.

"It's your recipe book. Instructions for a few activities that will help you work through each of the things we discussed. The copies aren't professional looking, but they can help you plan and implement each of the ingredients we talked about today..."

Greg held up the envelope and nodded his thanks. It wasn't thick, but he could tell there were some papers inside, and was curious to look inside and read them.

"So, you guys are probably ready to get on the road," Sophia continued. "Just remember . . . Goals determine and clarify team direction and priorities, relationships are connections that provide support, expectations are work agreements based on skills and strengths, accountability is empathy that inspires personal action, and toasts are recognition for efforts you want to see repeated."

"We won't forget them, Sophia," Cory promised.

Sophia patted Walt on the shoulder. "I've had lots of clients. Athletes, businessmen, teachers, coaches, and even nurses. But the recipe you learned today goes beyond the walls of where you work. Families are teams as well. They use the exact same process to build great teams."

"But knowing isn't doing," Sophia repeated. "You don't win games or build a business with knowledge alone. Knowing the right thing to do is easy. Doing it is what determines your progress. "Life is just a series of rapids that you will need to navigate with your team. And that is where my last gift to each of you comes in…"

"Last gift? I thought you just gave that to Greg?" Tricia said.

Sophia reached down into her backpack and pulled one last thing from her bag of tricks.

"Are those horseshoes?" asked Andy.

That is what they looked like. They were on key-chains. Sophia gave one to each of them. They were metal and about the size of a quarter.

"Are they to wish us good luck?" Greg questioned.

"No . . . wishing for luck is what you do, when you're not willing to work. These aren't for luck," Sophia answered.

"Looks a bit like a magnet." Susan commented, examining the one Sophia had given her.

"Well, magnets can draw things to them . . . but that's not it," Sophia explained

"I knew a guy that got kicked standing behind a horse one time. Are these supposed to remind us to give our people a kick when they need one?" Cory joked.

"You probably saw one of these when you talked to Patterson, Greg." Sophia explained.

"Yeah – he had a lapel pin, kind of like this. I didn't know what it was for," Greg answered.

"He keeps one on the wall in his office, too. Always has. I thought he was a fan of horse racing when I first saw it. But it wasn't there for luck. Or for kicking peo-ple...," Sophia raised her eyebrows and smirked in Cory's direction.

"It was there to remind him," Sophia continued, "and now to remind you guys, who is responsible for your team becoming a great one. Everything we have done today is meaningless without this...." She held up her hand, and they saw that she had one just like theirs as her own personal keychain.

"Well, horseshoes support and protect horses from harsh working conditions. Are these a reminder to keep us focused on supporting each other?" Tricia inquired.

"Nice guess, but that's not entirely it, either," Sophia answered.

"Okay . . . we give . . . what are they for, then?" Greg pleaded.

"You."

"No – the letter U. You decide whether your team has a compelling goal and the right gear to accomplish it. You determine whether your team has built rapport and strengthen their relationships. You are responsible for whether your team knows what is expected of them and if they encourage each other with reminders or deliver rearview mirror criticisms. You can be somebody that measures and publishes what's important and holds people accountable or helps the team make adjustments."

Cory leaned back from the picnic table and nodded his understanding.

Greg and the others were still motionless, listening.

"You choose what will get rewarded and recognized and celebrated, and what skills and memories people will eventually leave with. You impact everything and everyone around you . . . and it isn't luck – good or bad – that determines your fate..."

Sophia continued, with emotion. "It's YOU that ultimately decides your path and how well you travel it . . . U matter, because you leave ripples on the water! The stuff we talked about today doesn't have any value unless you choose to act on it..."

She stopped talking and gave them a moment to process her final lesson.

"U is also the mathematical symbol representing a union," Susan added.

"Wow – I didn't know that, Susan . . . Thanks!" Sophia smiled and put her keys back in her red backpack. Before she looked up, Greg rose from the picnic table bench to walked over and thank her.

"I don't know what I expected," he said, "but today . . . well, it has really been great!"

CHAPTER 12

ROWING TOGETHER

THE RIDE BACK TO Nashville was relatively quiet.

The group was exhausted and thoughtfully processing the day's events.

They shared a few laughs and talked about their time on the water together, but then Cory rested his head on the window and slept through part of it, and the others made occasional calls to update their family on the group's anticipated arrival time back home.

It was at a gas station, when they had stopped to refuel and grab a few snacks and drinks that Greg first opened the manila envelope that Sophia had handed him.

Inside the envelope was a hand written note to him and a handful of papers that had clearly been duplicated using on an old copier.

The note read:

"Dear Greg –

I am so thankful that we had a chance to spend the day together. You and your group will be able to use the ideas and activities on the pages in this packet to take action and start building your great team at CDI.

As I said at the picnic table, it is amazing how much you can change in one just day . . . but one day does not change things. One day just provides a catalyst that can cause you to see things differently – and that improved awareness, paired with different behaviors, changes things.

The five part recipe that we discussed on the water will help you and your people both at work and at home, and the papers in this packet share some activities you can use to clarify your thinking and create a GREAT culture.

If I can be a resource for you or one of your teams in the future, just let me know!

All My Best,
Sophia Mitchell"

Behind the note, Greg had found a stack of handouts that dealt with implementing the ingredients they had discussed.

He took a closer look at the papers and read through the activities, the following morning in the Nashville CDI offices, after getting everyone home.

By the time Greg arrived home and walked inside to hug his wife, it was after 10 p.m.

Lisa had dozens of questions, and he answered them as well as he could. He explained everything, from their first meeting with "Mitch" to the picnic table talk and the things she had told them and given them along the way.

On Friday morning, Greg woke up early and was the first person in the CDI offices.

He texted Mr. Patterson to thank him for the trip and asked him to call and talk when he could. Then, he sent out an email to every employee at the Nashville location to announce a meeting for that afternoon at three o'clock.

And then he opened up the envelope again to read through the papers more carefully.

There was an activity for setting goals and clarifying your team purpose.

There were a couple of ideas on how to improve engagement and help build relationships and improve interactions between the coworkers.

There was an activity for setting the expectations and suggestions on how to encourage people and have productive feedback conversations.

And there was an activity to allow people to identify their preferred type of recognition.

Each of the parts of their day together were covered – but the most important thing, Greg had picked up from Sophia was not an activity. It was the awareness that how he was leading affected the morale and pro- ductivity of the people he influenced.

Greg was sitting at his desk, and reached into his pocket to take out the key ring that he had just re- ceived as a gift the day before.

As he held it, he saw J.D. walk into the building.

"Greg stood up and walked over to his office door to call out.

"J.D., could you come and meet me in my office for a moment?" Greg placed the new key ring on his desk.

The two men hadn't spoken since the incident a couple of days ago.

J.D. walked unsurely into his boss' office. It was ob- vious that he didn't know what to expect from Greg.

"J.D.," Greg said, pointing to a chair. "Why don't you have a seat? I wanted to call you last night, but it was pretty late when I got in. We had a pretty interesting day yesterday as a management team, and before I meet with the entire staff this afternoon, I wanted to discuss a few of the changes we're making with you."

J.D. Cornett was a good salesman, and had been at CDI for years. He usually had an innate ability to read people and anticipate their moods or objections well enough to answer them and turn a conversation to his desired outcome.

At that moment, though, he was not reading Greg correctly at all.

"Greg, I know you've got a job to do. You're re- sponsible for making sure we are profitable, and I understand you were upset the other day..., but I do NOT think that one bad day is a cause for you to fire me!"

"What," Greg asked.

"I said I don't think you should..."

"I heard you. No, J.D. I'm not firing you!" Greg assured him. "I'm apologizing. You know, I've been here almost two years, and I don't know much about you at all. I know your numbers... Heck, I know everybody's numbers. I've done a great job of measuring those. But I've done a very bad job of everything else . . ."

J.D. adjusted himself in the chair and sat up straighter.

"No, Greg. It's okay. Really..." J.D. didn't know what to say.

Greg wanted to explain himself better. "We need metrics. But we need a lot more than that to be the company I want us to be."

J.D. nodded, and kept listening.

"And you are the first person I wanted to meet with personally," Greg said. "I wanted to let you know that I have a better idea now than I did a few days ago about what we need to do to be successful. And the thing that needs to change most is me. I got off to a rough start this first eighteen months or so, but I am really excited about growing this team. I just want you to know that I appreciate you being here."

Greg got up and reached his hand out.

J.D. sighed, stood to shake hands with him, and smiled . . .

"It's okay, Greg." He hesitated before asking, "You follow Duke Basketball?"

"A little . . . why?" wondered Greg.

"Well, Coach K got off to a rough start, too. You know he had a losing record his first three years there?"

"No . . . didn't know that J.D." Greg replied.

"Yeah. It's true. He never finished higher than fifth place in the ACC those first few years. Since then, though, he won three national championships, went to the final four seven times, and has won over a thousand games. He turned out alright," J.D. said. "I bet we will, too."

J.D. left his office, and Greg sat down just as the phone rang.

"Hello?"

"Greg . . . Matthew Patterson. I got your text. So the trip went well, did it?"

"Yes, it did, Mr. Patterson. Sophia . . . Mitch was terrific."

"Glad to hear it. So did you learn anything?"

"Yes we did. We learned a lot. More importantly, we are meeting today to discuss what we need to start doing differently."

Patterson paused on the other end of the line before speaking again.

"And what is it that you think needs to be different, after spending a day on the water with your people and with Mitch?"

Greg grabbed the key ring from his desk and help it up as he answered.

"The answer is U... I mean me!" He said, and laughed. "I mean, Sophia told us about the horseshoe pin you wear. I know it's me that sets the tone and influences our company culture, and I need to focus on all five parts of that recipe she told us about . . . but I probably need to build better relationships more than anything."

"I'm glad the trip was a success. Greg. Let me know if there's ever anything I can help you with from here. I look forward to hearing about your progress..."

"Yes, sir," Greg said, and then hung up his phone.

Their company was going to be different. He had the recipe for success.

No more underachieving!

No more poor communication!

No more bad connections!

From now on, they are gonna be GREAT.

APPENDIX

SOPHIA'S APPLICATION ACTIVITIES

Having purchased this book, if you are interested in "Looking through Mitch's Backpack" of How-to Handouts to help your team work through each step, you can find the link to those Leadership Resources at the bottom of the page **www.RapidTeamwork.com**

Once you register on Sean's site, you will be sent a password that gives you access to over 50 activities to develop and transform your group into a team!

• GOALS AND GEAR

• RAPPORT AND RELATIONSHIPS

• EXPECTATIONS AND ENCOURAGEMENT

• ACCOUNTABILITY AND ADJUSTMENTS

• TOASTS AND TRANSFER

ABOUT THE AUTHOR

Sean Glaze inspires people to have fun laughing together so they can have more success working together. His two books, *The Unexpected Leader* and *Rapid Teamwork* are powerful parables for building and leading great teams!

As a successful basketball coach and educator for over 20 years, Sean gained valuable insights into how to develop winning teams, and founded Great Results Teambuilding to share those lessons...

Today, he travels around the country delivering customized team workshops, facilitating fun team building events, and sharing entertaining and interactive conference keynotes that transform employees into **winning teammates**!

Made in the USA
Middletown, DE
22 September 2015